I0762785

Praise for

JAPAN, BEYOND THE GENKAN

"Joshua Walker offers many important insights, with affection and appreciation, about Japan itself and on US-Japan relations. He makes a powerful case for the importance of strengthening US-Japan relations and greater Japanese leadership on the world stage."

MERIT E. JANOW, chairman of Japan Society and Mastercard; dean emerita and professor, Columbia University

"*Japan, Beyond the Genkan* is a timely reminder that bridges between nations are built by people—through cultural curiosity, shared values, and human connection. My uncle, John D. Rockefeller III, devoted his life to strengthening US–Japan understanding through institutions like Japan Society and the Asian Cultural Council, which I continue to support as well. Joshua Walker admirably carries that legacy forward for a new generation, offering a compelling vision for the future of this essential alliance."

DAVID ROCKEFELLER JR., honorary chair, Asian Cultural Council

"US–Japan relations sit at the center of global security and democratic resilience in the Indo-Pacific. In *Japan Beyond the Genkan*, Joshua Walker illuminates why this alliance is not simply diplomatic—it is personal, political, and defining for the century ahead. His perspective, shaped by deep experience in both countries, shows how trust and human connection can strengthen deterrence, shape policy, and uphold shared democratic values. This is essential reading for leaders navigating the new geopolitical landscape.

JAMES KONDO, chairman, International House of Japan

"Dr. Walker's highly compelling book serves as a perfectly timed and strategically placed framing device for this moment in the US-Japan alliance. I encourage my fellow Americans—torn asunder by division—to learn from his poignant, textured descriptions of the vital Japanese concepts of *kizuna* and *omotenashi*. On a personal level, having now peeked beyond the *genkan*, I'm significantly more eager to strengthen the cultural bridges that my father, his father, and his father alike each helped build with their Japanese contemporaries."

JUSTIN ROCKEFELLER, executive chairman, Avenera

JAPAN, BEYOND *the* GENKAN

An Insider's Guide to the Soft Power, Strong Market, and Social Harmony of America's Asian Partner

JOSHUA W. WALKER, PhD

www.amplifypublishinggroup.com

Japan, Beyond the Genkan: An Insider's Guide to the Soft Power, Strong Market, and Social Harmony of America's Asian Partner

For more information, please contact:
Amplify Publishing, an imprint of Amplify Publishing Group
620 Herndon Parkway, Suite 220
Herndon, VA 20170
info@amplifypublishing.com

Library of Congress Control Number: 2026901763

CPSIA Code: PRV0126A

ISBN-13: 979-8-89138-790-4

Printed in the United States

To Grandpa Walker and Grandaddy Graham—without whom this story would not exist—and for my children, Jack and Macy, whose light gives my life meaning and the future its promise.

This book is dedicated to my family, whose story is intertwined with the long arc of US-Japan relations and also gives me the greatest sense of optimism for the future. To my grandfathers, Carlon Walker, Sr., and Dr. Lewis Graham, who served in World War II and whose exemplary service set into motion more than eighty years of familial ties to Japan, tracing the extraordinary journey from adversaries to allies. To my parents, Carlton and Cornelia Walker, who have devoted nearly half a century to life and service in Japan, quietly embodying the enduring bonds between our nations. To my children, Jack and Macy, who carry this story forward into a new generation of promises and possibility. And to my wife, Megan—my truly better half, my anchor, and my greatest strategic ally—whose love has sustained me at every step.

CONTENTS

PART TWO
GROWING UP BETWEEN JAPAN AND AMERICA:
LEARNING TO BECOME A GLOBAL BRIDGE-BUILDER

PART THREE
REIMAGINING LEADERSHIP:
PRESCRIPTIONS FOR JAPAN'S GLOBAL ROLE AND THE ALLIANCE'S FUTURE

FOREWORD

We are living in an era when the global balance of power is shifting faster than ever—and a moment when the tools of influence are no longer measured only in the firepower of armies or the growth of economies. In this fragmented "G-Zero" world, soft power has become a crucial currency of global leadership.

Joshua W. Walker's *Japan, Beyond the Genkan* captures this transformation through the lens of Japan—one of the most quietly influential nations of our time. I know from personal experience that no one understands the dangers created by a lack of coherent global leadership better than the elected leaders, business-decision-makers, and thoughtful citizens of Japan. They live on the frontlines of G-Zero conflict, caught between competing American and Chinese visions of the future. They know the vulnerabilities that come from deep connection to globalized trade and investment flows. They understand the potential of soft power to provide the strength and resilience that Asia and the world so badly need.

I've known Josh Walker for years. He helped lead our Japan relationships at Eurasia Group and we together created the GZERO Summit Tokyo, which I'm proud to say has become one of Asia's premier geopolitical gatherings. That event, born with Josh's vision and cultural fluency, brought together Japan's most senior political and business leaders to discuss how the world's power vacuum could also become an opportunity for renewed leadership.

As readers of this book will see, Josh's greatest asset isn't just his analytical mind or command of Japanese—it is his ability to connect values to strategy, people to policy, and ideas to action. This book extends that bridge from US-Japan relations to the wider world.

JAPAN'S ROLE IN A G-ZERO WORLD

When I first introduced the concept of the "G-Zero," I described a global system where no single power—not even the United States—could shape outcomes on its own. A decade later, G-Zero is now the water we all swim in. The United States has become more polarized, China more assertive, and Europe more preoccupied with challenges close to home. Amid this volatility, Japan has emerged as a model of stability, trust, and insightful leadership.

Where the United States often projects influence through hard power and China through economic leverage, Japan leads through credibility, culture, and consistency. From anime and architecture to business ethics and hospitality, Japanese soft power resonates globally because it is rooted in enduring human values: humility, harmony, respect, and reliability.

In the Trump era—marked by transactional diplomacy, erratic policy, and uncertain alliances—Japan's reliability has become even more valuable. As the emergence of Japan's first female prime minister in Takaichi and her engagement of President Trump reveals, *soft power has become Japan's strongest form of diplomacy*, not only complementing United States influence but in some areas also substituting for it.

As Josh notes in these pages, this isn't just a cultural export—it's strategic statecraft. Japan's ability to inspire trust gives it access and influence where hard power is unable to stand alone.

GEOPOLITICAL REALITIES

Japan sits today at the crossroads of nearly every major geopolitical battle line. Between the United States and China, it remains one of the very few advanced democracies capable of bridging the economic and security divide between the world's two largest powers.

Tariffs, technology restrictions, and reshoring debates have redrawn global trade maps. The international economic order faces its most significant round of disruption under President Trump and America First—one that will continue to test alliances as much as markets. In this environment, Japan's diplomatic agility and strategic restraint will be more important than ever.

At the same time, Tokyo is reassessing its own defense posture. With rising regional threats and expectations from Washington, Japan's commitment to increase defense spending marks a new era—one that blends soft-power credibility with credible deterrence. The challenge will be maintaining Japan's reputation as a peaceful nation even as it expands its hard-power capabilities.

Beyond East Asia, Japan has positioned itself deftly in the Middle East and multilateral institutions like the United Nations and G7. Its energy diplomacy, humanitarian aid, and commitment to sustainable development have earned respect across political divides. In a moment when few nations are trusted by all sides, Japan's balance of empathy and engagement stands out.

JAPAN AS AN EXPORTER OF VALUES

For much of my career, I have studied America's projection of power. Yet, the world today is looking not for dominance but dependability. Influence built on pressure cannot last; influence built on respect endures.

That's what makes Japan unique. When Washington wields pressure, Tokyo builds partnerships. Where Beijing seeks control through dependency, Japan offers reliability through quality and fairness. In this way, Japan's "quiet power" is proving a welcome addition to America's once-unquestioned "attractive power" and China's increasingly assertive global rise.

Josh Walker captures this moment brilliantly. His voice is both analytical and personal—combining the insight of a policy expert with the empathy of someone who grew up inside the culture he describes. Through that dual lens, he helps readers understand why Japan's values—its patience, integrity, and sense of harmony—matter not just in Asia, but to the entire world.

FINAL THOUGHTS

Japan, Beyond the Genkan is more than a book about Japan. It is a meditation on how nations lead when power itself is redefined. By reframing Japan's soft power as a form of geopolitical capital, Josh offers a guide for how trust and values can reshape international relations in an age of uncertainty.

His insights remind us that alliances are not only written in treaties—they're built in relationships. And as the world confronts new tests of resilience, Japan's example offers hope: that quiet strength and moral clarity still matter.

This book invites us to learn from Japan—not just about policy, but about purpose.

IAN BREMMER

President and founder, Eurasia Group
New York

INTRODUCTION

HOW TO ENSURE WE SUSTAIN 120 YEARS OF JAPANESE-AMERICAN CONNECTIONS FOR ANOTHER CENTURY

I am a bicultural and bilingual American—America is my homeland and Hokkaido, Japan, is my heartland. I grew up in Japan, where I learned to see America from the outside, and much later I became the ultimate insider in Washington, DC, and New York. Today, I am the youngest president and CEO of Japan Society in New York City, which will be 120 years old on May 19, 2027.

OUTSIDER/INSIDER

In this book, I examine the US-Japan relationship through the lens of my own life and experience as both an outsider and an insider, with the aim of bridging further understanding between Japan and the United States of America. Today the US-Japan alliance is more fragile than ever before in the last eighty years since the end of World War II, yet in a broader historical context of the 150 years of bilateral relations this uncertainty may just become the norm. In the last eighty years

America and Japan have always been there for each other through natural disasters, terrorist attacks, and regional wars.

In 1906, President Theodore Roosevelt won the Nobel Peace Prize for helping to end the Russo-Japanese War, and it was that war that brought Japan into the global system as a sovereign nation. Japan Society, founded in 1907, led the way in showcasing the abundance of Japan to an American audience. During World War II, when the US and Japan became mortal enemies, the Society wasn't destroyed or disbanded but rather went dormant.

After the war, the Society was transformed from a competitive chamber of commerce to an arts and cultural institution fostering true people-to-people exchange. Today, the global system is changing faster than ever before and connections between America and Japan must go beyond hard security, politicians, and even national bounds, to the truly human bonds represented by the Japanese word for spiritual connection: *kizuna*. To fully appreciate the value of the relationship and understand where and how it can evolve we must start with a single life lived on the intersection of the US and Japan with its myriad and complex connections.

In choosing to share my own story here, I am fully embracing my *ikigai* (a Japanese word meaning calling or purpose in life) as a bridge-builder between the US and Japan. For anyone who cares deeply about the relationship between Japan and the United States, whether that interest is personal, cultural, or professional, my hope is to open new paths for understanding beyond the traditional US-Japan bilateral narrative in a world that is becoming more uncertain and increasingly dangerous.

No matter what any person's political viewpoint or any leader's personal agenda is, we are all called upon as citizens to be actively involved in our own democracies and societies.

Nonprofits such as Japan Society—whose mission is to connect the peoples, cultures, and societies of the United States and Japan in a global context—are essential in working outside of the government to nurture people-to-people relationships in both the business and cultural arenas. Unlike when Japan Society was founded in 1907 or reconstituted after World War II, when we were the first and only resource for Japanese business, education, film, performing arts, or visual arts outside of Japan, now every major institution here in New York, from Carnegie Hall to Lincoln Center to the Metropolitan Museum of Art, features Japanese artists and content.

GOING BEYOND THE *GENKAN*

But there's more. This book—and my own journey—takes you beyond the *genkan* into an insider's view of Japan. In Japan, the *genkan* is the semi-public entrance or threshold leading to the private space within a house, where guests are received and exchange their shoes for slippers to be worn inside. Time in a *genkan* is a transitionary period when one is going from the outside to the inside. There is no equivalent word in English, because the closest match, lobby, is actually a fully public space, whether in an office building or an apartment complex. And in the United States, most houses do not have a lobby, or even a place to take off your shoes.

Today, going beyond the *genkan* to connect the individuals who build community across cultures matters now more than ever, especially in the US-Japan context. As the president and CEO of an institution that has stood the test of time and has worked with every president and prime minister since 1907, I know that Japan Society will weather the current moment. But as a leader, I feel compelled to speak out now. And there's an urgency through which I experience that need. This book is based on my personal experience as a global citizen working in the US-Japan space and it reflects my own deeply held convictions and opinions, which are not necessarily those of Japan Society or its board.

Today, we are living through a moment where the US-Japan relationship that began eighty years ago after the end of World War II must be fundamentally recast—because the world in which that alliance was developed and brought to fruition no longer exists. A significant period of history for US-Japan is coming to an end, and in some ways, this book is the opening chapter for what lies ahead. It's not just how today's leaders have transformed themselves that is reshaping the world, something has changed from the time that my grandfathers were fighting against Japan and even at the moment that I assumed the leadership of Japan Society in late 2019.

There will always be the historical point of view—the rhythms and cadences of history, the history of Japan Society, my own family history, and my own viewpoints that inform and speak to what might come next. I'm not writing this book as a journalist or an academic. I'm writing as someone who is deeply committed to the US-Japan relationship, as a person who has lived and continues to live this relationship through my life. I'm writing for everyone who cares deeply about US-Japan, for the future of that relationship in a new world where, by better understanding each other's cultures and societies, by going beyond the *genkan*, we can take that knowledge and make the world a better place for our children and those to come.

The election of Sanae Takaichi as the first female prime minister of Japan marks not only a historic milestone for her nation but also a moment that crystallizes the themes of this book. As a protégé of the late Prime Minister Shinzo Abe, she embodies both continuity and change, stepping into global summitry and her very first meeting of a world leader with President Trump at a time when the stakes for the US-Japan alliance could not be higher.

Yet the story of Japan cannot be understood only through the headlines of political leaders and diplomatic drama. To truly grasp Japan's place in the world—and what it means for America—we must go beyond the *genkan*, past the threshold of surface impressions, and into the deeper currents of culture, history, and people-to-people ties that define this enduring relationship.

PART ONE

SHARED IDENTITIES

Historical Lenses on US-Japan National Identities

CHAPTER ONE

TENDING OUR JAPANESE AND AMERICAN HOUSES

With all things related to Japan, there is the *tatemae*, which is the front face of any structure or story. Then there's the *honne*, which is going behind the scenes for the truth. The best analogue for this distinction might be the architecture of a Japanese house. First, there's a *genkan* or lobby where you walk in and you're greeted, and you take off your shoes. I think that many Americans who experience Japan only experience the lobby, the *genkan* of the country, like a beautiful Japanese meal or a visit to Kyoto or Tokyo. They only get past the front entrance without knowing that there's an inner part beyond the *genkan* which can be as enchanting as the *monozukuri*—the crafts and products of Japan that have become world famous, from Nintendo to Toyota. Of course, in Japanese culture it is much less common to invite someone to one's home than it is in the United States, so even making it into the *genkan* is to be celebrated. The *genkan* itself is ornate by nature, complete with intentionality and symbolism.

Then there's someone like myself, who grew up in Japan as both an outsider and an insider. I think my own journey and experience as an American growing up in a remote part of Japan tells a story that's as relevant as, for example, *Shōgun*, where an outsider becomes the ultimate insider. This is a story that happens throughout Japanese history because, ultimately, it takes a very long time to get past the entrance especially given the complexity of Japanese culture and language. One has to be able to step inside in an appropriate way. Unlike some cultures I've experienced, from German to Middle Eastern, Japanese will never correct or directly contradict you, rather they will gently and subtly teach you through what is not being said or the silence that they employ. Ironically, once we are inside we often don't think to tell the full story to the outside because by then the house itself is so much a part of our lives that we don't see its value beyond our own stories. We have to leave the house to tell our stories.

JAPANESE AND AMERICAN PERSPECTIVES

Japanese businesspeople, often referred to as "salarymen," are not supposed to think above their pay grades. They are meant simply to implement. That worked really well in the 1980s, when the economy was going gangbusters and the Japanese approach—defined by *kaizen*, or the belief in continual self-improvement—was working like a well-oiled machine. But when the outside world intervenes and there are geopolitical disruptions, whether it's the stock market in the 1990s, or war, or major disasters like the Great East Japan Earthquake of March 11, 2011 (known in Japan as 3.11), Japan needs to adapt. For that, the country needs guidance.

One of my goals here is for the Japanese themselves to understand that they have agency. In many ways, Japanese tend to be fatalistic about the world around them because they live in a precarious position. For one, their archipelago lies on the fault lines of tectonic plates, making them vulnerable to earthquakes and tsunamis. Also, their geographic position—off the coast from China and Russia, both increasingly more powerful—puts them adjacent to some of the most volatile power shifts in the world. Japanese think of their history in terms of divine winds, or *kamikaze*. Invasions from the Asian mainland or dominance from Europe or America have in the past comprised these winds. Japan has thus had to choose its allies and destiny carefully, even as Japanese seem to think things happen to them rather than as a result of their agency.

Americans, on the other hand, believe in shaping their destiny. Japanese businesspeople, and the business elites of Japan—often termed "Japan, Inc."—need to know that they can shape the world and their narrative just like the "American Dream" that feels less accessible to my generation of Americans than ever before. That was the big conversation back in the 1980s, largely conducted in economic terms as Japan, Inc., bought up American landmarks from Columbia Pictures to Rockefeller Center, but Japan's role is slightly different today. While US Steel is the most recent economic acquisition by Japan, it was in partnership with the American company and government that it was approved. In the West, particularly in the last decade in Silicon Valley, it is Japanese ideas of work that have most taken hold, particularly *ikigai* (life purpose) and *kaizen* (continual improvement). Examples from Okinawa to Toyota have been popularized with these terms without being fully grounded in the historic and ancient civilization that is true Japan or the Japanese language. The Japanese themselves are often skeptical of these words. These are words that I will also be using in this book, but not in the usual way people in the West use them.

I don't purport to know everything about Japan—in some ways, as I've learned the hard way many times before, the more you think you know about Japan, the more foolish you become. When you think about all the great Japanese leaders, whether in the Buddhist tradition, or the martial arts, or even in terms of policy and politics, no one can claim to be the ultimate master of Japan. Rather than the "great man" theory of leadership that often dominates the West, there is a great philosophy or *do* (translated as the "way") approach of deep intentionality and philosophy that very much defines Japan. So whether it is the way of the warrior, *bushido*, or tea, *chado,* that might be seen as opposed to each other in the West, they are grounded in the same philosophical underpinnings that make Japan Japan. As a result, many Japanese leaders simply take their own lived experience less as an inspiration to their followers and more as fellow travelers whom they hope to elevate, so that those who follow in their footsteps will be that much better off in a very incremental way. Similar to the footpaths to the top of Mount Fuji, the exact route is less important than the continual progress upward and the final destination that can be frustratingly circuitous to Americans. That's not grandiose in the American sense of the word, but it is an opportunity for those who may not even know they are following in their footsteps to intentionally look within, as I, too, hope to be doing.

LEARNING HOW TO DEAL WITH AMERICA

Japanese business leaders do have agency and the key to implementing this is learning how to deal with America—Japan's most important ally, its most important market, and one of its biggest influencers. This will allow the Japanese to feel more secure, and to feel confident in the role they have to play. There are many Americans, not just myself, who have benefited tremendously from the successes of Japan, not just Japan's economic successes but its cultural successes. It hasn't always been that way—I know this from my own life and also through my family legacy.

It is useful to be able to see both sides. There is no right or wrong experience. There are many Americans who have had amazing experiences in Japan, but I want to help people who want to go beyond the *genkan* to experience the abundance of Japan that I've had throughout my life. Part of this is about Japan Society's mission. It's the reason I took on the leadership of this organization, knowing all of the challenges that I would face but also just how valuable the journey could be. I hope that in some ways I can leave a little part of myself so that others don't have to make some of the mistakes I have, but, at the same time, so that I can celebrate the people who have been with me along the way. Because this isn't just my own personal story, it's the story of a much larger group of people—from my family, to the staff at Japan Society, to the amazing individuals whose cross-cultural connections with Japan and the US are shaping history.

CHAPTER TWO

A SOCIETY THAT SYMBOLIZES A CENTURY-LONG PARTNERSHIP

In this time where knowledge and being up to date on what's happening in the world is so critical, Japan Society is well positioned to serve as an essential resource. Founded in 1907 by American business leaders and Japanese living in New York City, Japan Society was born at the Hotel Astor in New York during a luncheon honoring General Kuruki Tamemoto, a visiting hero of the Russo-Japanese War. Although its mission of connecting American and Japanese peoples, cultures, and societies has remained consistent, Japan Society is naturally driven by the forces of history and geopolitics. As Richard Wood, the Society's president during its centennial, wrote in the 2007 introduction to the Society's centennial history book: "At the time of the Society's beginning in 1907, little could the first founding directors have known what a broad-sweeping and enduring enterprise they were creating. The 'long and successful health' wished upon the Society by General Kuroki at the founding luncheon on May 19, 1907, has been translated into more than a hundred years of cultural and intellectual interface between the United State and Japan."

Japan Society began as a business association and an industrialists' club of the Who's Who in elite American circles who predicted that Japan's meteoric rise would be beneficial to their own country. Of course, it didn't end there. The Society was shut for the duration of the Pacific War, when the US and Japan brought horrific suffering and devastation upon each other—suffering which only ended when America dropped atomic bombs on Hiroshima and Nagasaki. Following the end of the American Occupation of Japan in 1952, the Society reopened under the brilliant leadership of John D. Rockefeller III, who focused on uniting the two countries through the universal language of arts and culture while also offering support to Japanese students and emerging artists from Japan who were living in New York City.

THE MAKING OF JAPAN HOUSE

In the late 1960s, interest expanded in both the culture and business acumen of Japan, putting programming space at a premium. After the Society's board determined that the organization needed its own headquarters, John D. Rockefeller III donated the land, located very close to the United Nations, for which his family had also gifted property, and funds for construction were raised equally between American and Japanese corporations. Japan House, Japan Society's now-landmarked building, opened to the public in September 1971 with Their Imperial Highnesses Prince and Princess Hitachi as honored guests. Architect Junzō Yoshimura stated at that time: "I hope that the House will play its full role in promoting understanding between the United States and Japan." Responding to Japan's emergence as a world economic power, in the years that followed Japan

Society came to be a leading New York cultural institution as well as a forum for Japanese and American business leaders.

The early Japan House years brought the full breadth of Japanese culture to New York. A new gallery flourished under the innovative leadership of its first director, Rand Castile, while Beate Sirota Gordon, who had been instrumental in ensuring women's rights in the drafting of Japan's postwar constitution, invigorated the Society's performing arts program. During this time, Japan Society paved the way in presenting to New York audiences the visual and performing arts of Japan, then considered niche by the Western world and which are now mainstreamed by major cultural institutions such as the Metropolitan Museum of Art, Carnegie Hall, and Lincoln Center. As time passed, others took the place of these early luminaries, who were not only an essential part of Japan Society's history but vital to the US-Japan story, as well as to American civilization and art.

WHAT JAPAN SOCIETY MEANS TO ME

To me, Japan Society is the full package. Through the sum of its storied history, it brings together everything in a way that few thinktanks, museums, universities, concert halls or centers for innovation can claim to do—not even the America-Japan Society in Tokyo or the International House of Japan, both of which Japan Society is very strongly connected to and which in many ways serve as our natural counterparts historically and culturally in Japan. Today, more than forty independent Japan-America Societies operate in the US, often staffed by volunteers and driven by mission rather than mandate and grouped loosely under the National Association of Japan-America Societies that Japan Society helped create as an umbrella organization and on whose executive committee I have sat since I became president.

Many of these Japan-America Societies and their corollary sister city partnerships emerged in the aftermath of World War II, when reconciliation and understanding were not abstractions but urgent necessities. Inspired by a desire to foster peace and mutual respect, these organizations focused not on policy, but on people-to-people diplomacy. Perhaps the most iconic sister city partnership is not the one between New York or Toyko or between San Francisco or Osaka but rather in America's and Japan's heartlands, between St. Paul, Minnesota, and Nagasaki, Japan. That partnership was formed in 1955, just a decade after the war. Since then, over 450 US cities have partnered with their Japanese counterparts, creating one of the most extensive and enduring networks of bilateral civic engagement in the world. In parallel, Japan-America Societies blossomed across the United States—from DC to Honolulu, Boston to Texas—promoting Japanese culture, language education, and cross-cultural understanding at the grassroots level.

When I took the job as the twentieth president of Japan Society my hope was to make the organization even more accessible to those beyond our neighborhood and to take our truly universal mission of connecting America and Japan global through partnerships and virtual programming to help the Society's almost 120-year story become an integral part of the future of US-Japan relations. I truly believe that institutions like Japan Society can become an integral part of the future of US-Japan relations by serving as a human backbone—connecting individuals, communities, and organizations in ways that transcend politics and policy, and grounding this critical alliance in trust, understanding, and shared purpose. While defense alliances and trade negotiations will always dominate headlines, it is institutions like the Japan Society along with our fellow Japan-America Societies and sister cities across the United States and Japan that form the connective tissue of the bilateral relationship. They operate not in embassies, but in school auditoriums and city halls. They don't issue communiqués—they issue invitations. And in doing so, they ensure that the US-Japan relationship is not just strategic—it's personal. In the face of geopolitical uncertainty and shifting public sentiment, Japan and America can look to these local institutions as models of what durable diplomacy looks like. Theirs are not quick fixes or grand gestures, but quiet persistence, rooted in friendship and mutual respect. Without them, the song of US-Japan relations would lose its most human notes.

Early on in my tenure I had no idea I would almost immediately confront a global pandemic that would physically shut down the organization for the first time since the outbreak of World War II. I took the job because I felt a collective sense of responsibility to the mission of this critical organization that was also deeply personal. As an American who grew up in Japan, I felt a unique sense of responsibility and a strange kinship with Japan Society even though I hadn't visited the organization before my formal appointment. And so, I uprooted my family and the life I knew in the greater Washington, DC, area to move to New York, where I was to learn what it means to be baptized by fire.

After the global pandemic shut down the world physically, those of us at Japan Society pivoted to enrich ourselves through virtual connections, sharing experiences and cultural values during that uncertain and unprecedented time. To me, that's what Japan Society represents—not only connecting American and Japanese peoples in New York, but also in Japan, and working with everyone who is a friend of US-Japan to further our mission. Whether in person or through a digital connection, Japan Society instills a spiritual component that lifts everyone up together.

For me, Japan Society is like that shining city on a hill that Ronald Reagan so famously spoke of. For America, Japan Society is the symbol of everything that Japan represents to the world today, having evolved from a niche culture to mainstream. My children have grown up watching the Macy's Thanksgiving Day Parade , which is as American as the apple pie we eat for dessert, and Pikachu and Dragonball, which are as much a part of their lives as Snoopy or Garfield.

For Japan, my role as the leader of this organization is that of a true friend with a unique ability to translate and bridge the gaps that exist between our cultures and societies. As we will explore, the Japanese tend to be more consensus-driven rather than individually focused Americans and more attuned to harmony rather than independently driven Americans. Japan's products and ideas have never been more in vogue and yet Americans still do not fully grasp the essence of Japan. And the Japanese themselves often are not the main beneficiaries as they themselves don't fully appreciate how popular they and their ways have become. I do not represent Japanese in America or Americans in Japan but rather I speak on behalf of our members both individual and corporate who have made Japan a part of their lives here in New York and in America more broadly. While my story is very much my own and I can only speak to those experiences I've had, as president of Japan Society I lift up the stories in the US-Japan community that inform and inspire us all.

CHAPTER THREE

SHIMAGUNI VERSUS TRANSFORMATION

History is cyclical. Every great opening comes with a great closing, and every closing leads to a new opening. In Japan, the Meiji Restoration began a period of globalization and expansion that ultimately led to World War II. The ending of the war, and with it that era of closure, was followed by a great re-opening and a period of growth and revitalization. This chapter examines two major periods in history—the Meiji Restoration and the American Occupation of Japan after World War II—when Japan was transformed from a *shimaguni*—a closed island nation, locked into its unique history and traditions—to a society and culture profoundly reshaped by outside influences. Additionally, the COVID pandemic isolated Japan once again and is still resonating throughout the world. Today we are at another critical turning point in history; we are going from the open society defined by globalization after World War II to a populist nativism that is reconsidering America and Japan's place in the world.

Change is inevitable, but how we respond to change, whether as societies or cultures, as collectives or individuals, is enhanced by a better understanding of the agents of transformation. It is *gaiatsu*, or outside pressure for change, rather than internal pressure, that usually moves Japan historically. With its deep *shimaguni* roots and cycles of history extending over thousands of years, Japan stands in direct contrast to the far younger and essentially linear history of the United States. Yet both of our countries need each other in order to evolve. Some may ask if America really needs any other country in the world to evolve, but, particularly in the interconnected economy and attention-driven culture Americans have come to enjoy, Japan stands out as America's single largest investor and one of the most popular sources of American's products, from cars and watches to anime and video games. By understanding our own strengths and weaknesses, and supporting each other through mutual understanding, we can make the most of this time of transformation, together.

OUTSIDER VS. INSIDER, AGAIN

It all goes back to outsider versus insider. An outsider is actually the ultimate insider. If you're an insider, you shouldn't be critiquing or criticizing, you should just exist. Whereas as an outsider, you might start out as a barbarian who comes in trying to force change, but over time, outsiders become like insiders, and insiders come to appreciate outsiders. That kind of fluidity is much more comfortable in a Japanese approach that's not black and white. This is why in Japan there is a very strict kind of protocol—first to prepare a person for being accepted and then to become an insider by moving beyond the *genkan* to the inner sanctum.

In the United States now we are going through a period of closure defined by blaming outsiders like undocumented immigrants for the woes of society that is directly impacting the global architecture once championed by America as its natural leadership role in the world. This is not quite the same as the physical closures that have locked down Japan over history, which is easier without any land borders like those being walled off in America's south—it is a closure in mindset. However, this closure is preparing us for a great opportunity of openness and understanding that the Japanese themselves are part of. Each of our societies need to accept that opportunity. Americans need to reach out and take agency to bring in the outsiders who can help us move beyond the closed mindsets that exist even with all the available technological connection.

SOCIETAL PATTERNING

In America, the desire to exclude those who are not like ourselves is reflected in the MAGA movement. Their ideology is one of "us versus them." In other words, "we are the insiders and you are outsiders who are not entitled to the full acceptance that every person who looks like me is entitled to." Let's not forget that many Americans today were the ultimate outsiders from Europe when they arrived at an insider's land that was already settled by Native Americans. It's contrary to American's own story to arbitrarily draw a line in 1776 and use a fifty-year window in defining who can and cannot be an American. That also ignores longer cycles of history—not only Asian but Western history.

In Japan the patterns of insider and outsider are very clearly defined. Whether or not the Japanese realize it, they are being taught about insider and outsider patterns through their culture and society. Even the three systems of writing in Japanese—*hiragana*, *katakana*, and *kanji*—illustrate a long tradition of outside influence. *Hiragana* is adapted from kanji, or Chinese characters, to fit the Japanese language and *katakana* was created for words that came from outside of Japan. In fact, certain words that are now thought of as native to Japan such as *anime* are actually foreign terms in *katakana* that have not only been appropriated but have also become among Japan's greatest exports. Americans are not taught the same way. We're taught that pretty much every one of us is unique and that history is less important than what we do, now and in the future. In Japan, you are taught that you are not that different from anybody else, and that what takes place has been done before. The juxtaposition between "*shimaguni*" and "transformation" doesn't really seem like a juxtaposition, but what happens when we look at when the greatest transformation occurs? The most exciting moment happens at the point between when a closed society opens up and when it starts to flourish. Ultimately, each of our respective societies will meet and evolve from that turning point that leads to transformation. Let's take a closer look at some of these earlier turning points in history.

THE MEIJI RESTORATION

The arrival of American Commodore Matthew Perry's Black Ships at Yokohama in 1853 effectively marked the beginning of the end of the Tokugawa Shogunate's rule in Japan and paved the way for the Meiji Restoration in 1868, the year that the Emperor Meiji, whose name means "enlightened rule," ascended to the throne. Although Japanese history is very long, from an American perspective the history of Japan doesn't really begin until 1853 with the arrival of Commodore Perry's Black Ships. Before then, Japan was a black box, an island nation that was closed off to America. Some Europeans, especially the Dutch, had been trading with the Japanese through Nagasaki, the only port open to foreigners and the one used by Europe, which had already divided up the rest of the world under various agreements and empires. But

Commodore Perry took his fleet directly into Yokohama, the nearest port to the capital city of Edo, bringing with him the message that he was going to open up Japan for America and to let him in or he would blow them all up. This was a clear declaration from the US to the Japanese emperor, who wasn't very strong because during the Tokugawa period it was the Shogunate that had the power. The Shogunate was a military government led by a shogun, who held real political and military power, while the emperor remained the symbolic and spiritual ruler of Japan with limited actual authority; in other words, the emperor reigned but the shogun ruled. This feature that has come to be associated with the Japanese can still be felt in modern-day power dynamics.

That forced opening jumpstarted the dissolution of what was already a very fragile system. That system had lasted far longer than it should have. It would have crumbled much earlier had there been earlier outside challenges to the Shogunate. The system did crumble, and not because American ships or American power were so strong but because there was a desire for change in Japan, and this was the first of many opportunities. In essence, the Americans became the tool of *gaiatsu*, the outside pressure for change, in which there was already an interest but no face through which to do it until the Black Ships came. The outsiders—the Americans—became a foil for the insiders to latch on to the outsiders, exposing the weaknesses of the once great traditional samurai families and samurai protectors, while a new and younger generation brought about the Meiji Revolution and the defeat of the ancient samurai regime. With a focus on modernization, in a very short period of time, some 600 years of Japanese history was demolished. Where only a few decades earlier foreigners had been seen as barbarians, the Japanese began to adopt aspects of the outside world into their own society such as Prussian military uniforms, the French system of justice, the Swiss legal code, and American agricultural methods.

GLOBALIZATION

As Japan began to globalize, America was the least threatening country because at that time it was not a superpower like Britain, France, Spain, or Portugal. Of all the outsiders, the Americans were the most entrepreneurial, and attractive to Japan because the US did not have a long history with imperialism and was in some ways still in reaction to it. Perhaps the Japanese saw a bit of a kindred spirit in America as a brand-new nation still wide-eyed and bushy-tailed about manifest destiny in the West. Americans began to work for Japan as paid mercenaries, and after a first internal war that led to a new consolidation of power, Japan began to wage a series of wars under its new "democratic" system and the ambiguously worded Meiji Constitution. Japan's Meiji Constitution was deliberately worded ambiguously to preserve imperial authority while appearing to adopt modern constitutional principles, allowing the government to justify authoritarian rule under the guise of legality and imperial will. The new Japanese government that replaced the shogunate sensed that something beyond the edict power of the emperor was needed. It wasn't just about military power, it was about sovereignty. For as Japan began to modernize, it became clear that a modern nation needed to have imperial states.

Japan conquered the Chinese first because China had already been weakened by the British Empire, taking for themselves the rump pieces such as Taiwan and the northern parts of Manchuria, then moving on to new conquests in Korea. But the *pièce de résistance* was the Russo-Japanese War of 1904-1905—the first time that war waged by Japan was not just Asian nation versus Asian nation but Japan against a European power. When the Russians sent their entire naval fleet the Japanese navy crushed them, bringing the strength of their navy to the attention of the Americans and the British, the two other big fleets in that part of the world. Ultimately it was President Theodore Roosevelt who mediated peace between the Japanese and the Russians. But if he had not stepped in, the Japanese might have kept going and probably would have taken a lot of more of Russia, including Vladivostok and much of Siberia.

MILITARIZATION

There are significant lessons to be learned from this period of history, which was fundamentally different from earlier periods when Japan's geography basically protected it from invasion and discouraged external aggression. When the Black Ships arrived, Japan began to learn that it needed cannons, gunpowder, and all the weapons of modern warfare. Japan was on a collision course with the other power in the region, which happened to be the United States, and the Sino-Japanese and Russo-Japanese Wars were both proofs of weaponry modernization and a prequel to the atrocities that happened in the lead-up to World War II.

At that time Japan had a weak democratic system that was rooted neither in the imperial court or the different families who had ruled previously. It was a constitutional authority that had basically been put together after Japan looked around at the rest of the world, especially Europe, and assumed that that was what was needed. The Japanese government, obsessed with *kaizen*—continuous self-improvement—began by rejecting Chinese culture and then declaring that they had to catch up with what was happening in other parts of the world. In earlier times, power in Japan had previously been defined by the amount of land that was controlled. After consolidating the Ainu populations in Hokkaido and subjugating the Ryukyu in Okinawa, the only way for Japan to increase its power was to move outside of the mainland, starting with Taiwan, Korea, and China, then moving on to Russia. Teddy Roosevelt prevented the last incursion. The rest of the world, however, was still up for grabs. World War I, during which Europe was decimated and Germany was divided up among the Allied Powers, was waged at a moment when Japan was the largest power in Asia. Japan, as one of the League of Nations countries after World War I, became the protector of many of the former colonies of those defeated powers, learning from its time in the international system that power was very much defined in military terms. That was not power gained by cultural influence or economic sphere, it was hard imperial power which Japan could exert beyond its mainland.

A BLUEPRINT FOR POWER

As globalization advanced, the United States emerged as a blueprint for Meiji Japan, inspiring its leaders to transform the nation into a modern, industrialized power with international influence and imperial ambitions. That, of course, was unrealistic with America being a continental power and Japan a small island nation. The United States controlled key natural resources, like oil and steel, that Japan desperately needed for its modernization, making America the primary obstacle to Japan's inevitable rise as a dominant power in Asia.

Japan attacked Pearl Harbor, thinking that the only way to be able to continue to rise as a military power was to take the resources it needed by force. There was also a major divide between the Japanese army and the navy. Unlike the US, where the armed forces are co-equal, in Japan the navy had historically been the driver of Japanese military policy as the most important branch of an island nation. But the Japanese army had been so successful during previous military campaigns that they insisted on attacking Pearl Harbor against the advice of the navy. From that point onward, a hard ending was inevitable.

Japan believed that America did not have much political drive, and if the American fleet in Pearl Harbor could be eliminated, it would take the US too long to recover and it would therefore be unable protect itself. Another significant miscalculation was in thinking that America's focus would be almost exclusively on the Atlantic sphere, and that Americans, who were predominantly European Americans, would not care too much about what happened in Asia. In some ways, the Japanese were right. America didn't enter the war in the Pacific to save the Asian people. But by attacking America Japan badly miscalculated and paid a very steep price. In looking at the US, the Japanese saw a divided country—but it was a country that would unify upon being attacked. Before Pearl Harbor the US had been doing its level best to stay out of the European conflict and ignore the atrocities that were happening there. It took one thing only to change that dynamic—and that was Japan.

Although there was technically Japanese "democracy" before World War II, Japan didn't have a strong constitution and the imperial and shogun top-down fascist military approach was still the law of the land that unified Japan. Unlike the US, which has had only one major civil war, Japanese history is rife with civil wars. When it is unified, however, there have been fewer civil wars. As a result, unification has manifested in a call to be unified against the outside world. Yet in the period when Japan's power was held by a number of individual *daimyo*, or warlords, they would trade with outsiders to effect a balance of power. Although Japan is basically a unified society, that is ironically in some ways a reaction to how divisive Japanese history has been since its beginnings, including its naturally restrictive geography. Unlike the expansive plateau region that allowed Genghis Khan to conquer all of Eurasia, Japan remained unconquered by anyone until the end of World War II. In this context, Americans don't use the word "conquer;" instead, we use "occupy," which is interesting because "embracing defeat" is a term that is also often used for Japan. The Japanese themselves accepted and wholeheartedly took their defeat in 1945 because they wanted to preserve the imperial system, whose ultimate meaning continues to be debated today.

THE OCCUPATION

Following Japan's surrender in 1945, the Occupation of Japan under General Douglas MacArthur as supreme commander for the Allied Forces from 1945 to 1952 set the path for the great reopening that brought about Japan's postwar renaissance. MacArthur had distinguished himself as a military genius in the Pacific Theater but his ultimate success in leading the Occupation was the way in which he seemed to understand Japan, not because he himself understood Japan, but because he hired advisors and experts who deeply understood the essence of Japan's culture and language, ensuring that the transformation of occupied Japan was guided by insight into its traditions, values, and societal structure.

Occupations are usually couched in terms of military rule and directive, but MacArthur also considered how he could partner with the people of Japan to America's advantage. He was the presence behind the idea of not removing the emperor, a consequential decision that ultimately led to the success of US-Japan relations. Japan's constitution, which MacArthur in many ways drafted and had the Japanese Diet pass, still remains in place eighty years after the end of the war. MacArthur allowed the Japanese to figure out what would work best for them and then put in place what America needed to make that happen. America wasn't that concerned about how the internal workings of Japan's economy were going to be played just as long as it meant success for the new US-Japan relationship.

At the same time, the United States began to shape its response to the threat of the Soviet Union, and Japan became critically important to the American side from a security perspective. MacArthur understood this better than anyone, and because of his high level of connectivity and respect in both countries he was able set democratic mechanisms in place that were not previously possible. Security, stability, and economic growth were the three pillars that led to Japan's economic rebirth between 1952 and 1964.

JAPAN'S ECONOMIC MIRACLE

Japan had to rebuild itself from the extreme devastation of a war that had been ended by the atomic bombings of Hiroshima and Nagasaki. Forty percent of Japan's urban areas had been destroyed, including sixty percent of Tokyo, where hundreds of thousands of Japanese civilians died, and at least eight million became homeless. The Treaty of San Francisco came into force on April 28, 1952, ending the Occupation and returning sovereignty to Japan. The next ten years of Japan's miraculous growth were made possible by the American security guarantee and by American investment in Japan. As the United States began to ramp up its war efforts first in Korea and then in Vietnam, Japan became a major beneficiary as well as a critical staging ground for US forces. Japan's economic growth and planning were fueled by the fact that the country didn't need to spend anything on its own security or militarization, which was prohibited under the new constitution.

Japan's economic miracle, a period of rapid economic growth that lasted until the early 1990s, began with the 1964 Tokyo Olympics, closely followed by the 1970 Osaka World Expo, whose theme was "progress and harmony for mankind." These previously Eurocentric milestones were the first of their kind to take place in Asia, shifting the center of gravity for global affairs. Japan's centerpiece at the 1964 Olympics was the Shinkansen, the bullet train that connected all of Japan to Tokyo and is still the envy of the world sixty years later. Even though held in the later years of the twentieth century, the Osaka Expo showcased the potential of the twenty-first century, especially the Space Race that was really just starting, exciting the imaginations of the Japanese with moon rocks on display in the USA Pavillion and bringing more visitors to the region than ever before.

Around the same time American investment in Japan began to burgeon. The Osaka Expo had done a great job of making Japan's largest trading hub more visible to the broader global community. Previously, America had been a global economic superpower that Japan had no hope of meeting on equal terms. American businesses now began to see the potential in Japan. Some of the fundamentals that make Japan an attractive economic engine today were beginning to present themselves—the dynamism of the Japanese economy lies in its ability to continuously adapt through innovation-driven industries like robotics and advanced manufacturing, a highly educated workforce, and strong coordination between government and business sectors especially relative to Europe, Japan's strategic importance to American interests, and the roots of the broader geopolitics from the China opening that was to take place under President Richard Nixon. Major Japanese companies including Toyota and Sony began selling to the American market, subsequently becoming dominant forces in their own right. Globalization between the US and Japan during this period saw both economies recognizing how interconnected they were becoming, and leaders on both sides understood that what happened on the New York Stock Exchange would be reflected in Tokyo the next day and vice versa. At the same time, the United States became increasingly aware of Japan as a cultural entity due to the postwar Occupation, rising academic interest, and growing exposure to Japanese arts, traditions, and aesthetics—ranging from Zen Buddhism and tea ceremony to literature and design—which sparked fascination with its unique blend of ancient heritage and modern identity.

COVID

In early March of 2020, the global COVID pandemic brought about forced closures and sweeping societal changes. And we're still feeling the impact. In the US, New York City was the epicenter of the deadly virus that was thought to have come from a lab in China—something that is still unconfirmed today. In America, the response to the emergency came under the jurisdiction of the individual states, meaning that the strict lockdown in New York City was very different than, for example, Florida, where lockdowns never really happened. Coincidently, I became president and CEO of Japan Society in late December 2019. I moved my family to New York the last week of February, a week before the shutdown started. For me, COVID is very much intertwined with the beginning of my own experiences of Japan Society, which was physically shut down for six months by New York City as everyone was forced to isolate at home. With our building open only for essential maintenance, all programming and work that historically had been done in person transitioned to online to serve a wider audience that was hungry for distraction from forced isolation. Japan Society was in a fight for survival along with the rest of the city's cultural institutions. Scars from that time, especially financial ones, remain.

The US began to reopen in the fall of 2020 after the worst of the pandemic had subsided and vaccines had become available. Japan, however, effectively shut itself off from the outside world for more than two years. No foreign visitors were permitted without a family connection and a mandatory two-week quarantine period. Using a very different calculation of risk-taking from the rest of the world, Japan closed itself off as much as possible to protect its entire population. Japan Society's work, which depends on direct, in-person connections between the US and Japan, was greatly affected, especially on the cultural side. Visual art exhibitions, film screenings, language classes, and public programs that showcase traditional and contemporary

Japanese culture while fostering mutual understanding and dialogue were impossible because no one was able to fly in from Japan. After I made the decision to host our annual fundraising event virtually, many other organizations took note and decided to do the same thing. We found that people would still donate for those events even though they could not meet physically. They were able to join and feel inspired by each other during the enforced period of isolation. But Japan stayed shut, and after about two years many, including those of us in America, felt compelled to speak out to begin what was ultimately a successful campaign to encourage its reopening. Japan's mentality as a *shimaguni*, its instincts of trying to protect people, was no longer to its benefit, and Japan was in real danger of falling behind places like South Korea and Taiwan that had successfully reopened earlier and reaped the benefits.

Today, societal changes from the forced COVID closures are ongoing, especially in the US, where remote learning has adversely impacted an entire generation of students, and populist anger and social unrest reflects the effects of isolation combined with frustration over government and leadership. Although Japan has physically recovered and reopened itself to the world, its insular mentality and consensus-driven society still put it at risk in today's globally driven world. The question today for Japan is, does it want to go back to its natural roots as a closed island nation or will it choose to compete in a global marketplace where its ideas and culture, as well as its products, are being acknowledged on a grand scale?

CHAPTER FOUR

NAVIGATING CRISIS TO OPPORTUNITY WITH JAPAN

Throughout every crisis that has confronted America in my lifetime, Japan has been one of the first countries to offer immediate and unconditional help. Whether that was something as formative for me as 9/11, when more Japanese perished than almost any other nationality besides Americans—given how closely linked our financial institutions and systems are in New York—or the most recent fires in Hawaii or California, where Japan and its people responded immediately and instinctively. I may be more naturally attuned to Japan's efforts given my background and connections, but I do believe there is much more that we as Americans can learn from Japan, whether in crisis or opportunity.

RESPONDING TO CRISIS

The English word "crisis" comes from the classical Greek word *krisis*, meaning "separation," implying at its root a separation or turning point. The Japanese write "crisis" as 危機 (*kiki*) from the Chinese characters, but when the two characters are separated, one is attributable to "danger" and the other to "opportunity," as President John F. Kennedy made famous through his speeches. This juxtaposition has been frequently discussed, misused and even overused, but it still matters. Perhaps it explains why I see crisis in the way that I do—rather than a crisis being something that is only dangerous and potentially destructive, I see crisis also as an opportunity and turning point. Even in the context of the English language, American politicians have spoken about not letting a crisis go to waste. In a time of crisis, ordinary people do extraordinary things because they are forced to respond in a totally different way.

Crises have the power to mobilize people and nations. After 9/11, one of the first leaders that President Bush talked to after the US military leaders was Japanese Prime Minister Koizumi, who offered his immediate support to America. Although Japan was and still is a pacifist nation, it was very unusual for Japan to go out on a limb in this way, but throughout every crisis that has confronted America, Japan has been one of the first countries to offer help. The 3.11 triple disaster was one of the few times that America could pay Japan's help forward and be present for the country in its moment of need. Not only were we there, but we met the moment and exceeded it. I don't want to see this goodwill squandered by our political leaders who may or may not be the ones representing that well of *kizuna* that has been built by the US-Japan friendship, or *tomodachi*.

CRISIS AND LEADERSHIP

Crisis is where the crucible of leadership lies and where a leader's true mettle comes to light. We can go for decades without a major crisis, and whether someone is a great political leader or not will never be known unless they have been tested. There's a not insignificant correlation with crisis for many of the leaders that we venerate the most in the US and Japan. A crisis is when you learn the most about people. But "crisis" is now being overused. It's somewhat like what's happening with "breaking news." In March 2011, broadcasts in the US were interrupted to announce the terrible disasters happening in Japan, but today breaking news consists of yet another presidential announcement that is deemed to be a crisis, around which people then try to justify their behavior.

There are different levels of crises. There is human crisis, which is an existential crisis. There's national crisis in terms of war and what might lead to the destruction of a country or an entire way of life. There are terrible things that happen that are not truly existential. When you add "existential" to crisis, that's how I understand true crisis—it's something that is life or death. Some types of disaster, like 3.11, cannot even be imagined. Although the nuclear facility in Fukushima was known to be located on a fault line and it was almost guaranteed that a major earthquake would occur at some point in time, insufficient preparations were made. The same can be said of other cities on fault lines such as Los Angeles, San Francisco, and Tokyo. During a major hurricane cities like New York will probably incur deaths from the loss of power and storm-related flooding. Especially with climate change, we're probably all going to experience something along these lines. Still, although we may not be able to fathom a particular crisis, we have to plan for it. Then there's the truly horrific—the atomic bombing of Japan in 1945 with a level of destructive capability that no one really understood but that we are capable of bringing about as human beings.

SHINZO ABE

The tragic assassination of former Prime Minister Shinzo Abe in July 2022 continues to cast a long shadow over Japan and its global role.

This singular event didn't have an enormous impact in the United States but a great deal of damage was done in Japan. As I wrote in an op-ed published in *Newsweek*, "In Shinzo Abe we lost a true friend of America and US-Japan relations." More importantly, the loss of Abe meant that the progress he enacted by moving beyond the Yoshida Doctrine was in peril. The Yoshida Doctrine saw weakness as a strength. But Abe solidified Japan's security alliance with the US, resulting in greater protection for its military bases and nuclear weapons. Abe reclaimed Japan's desire to stand on its own two feet not in opposition but in partnership with America. He projected Japan firmly on the global stage, whether dressing up as Super Mario in Rio to help win the Olympics for Tokyo or by standing between glaring European leaders and President Trump in one of the most famous G7 photos of all time. Abe's assassination was the loss of a true internationalist who has not yet been replaced. But most of Japan's political elites have been shaped and touched by him in some way.

Abe had a unique political legacy as the grandson of Nobusuke Kishi, who served as the prime minister from 1957 to 1960 and signed the Treaty of Mutual Cooperation and Security between the United States and Japan. He was also the son of Shintaro Abe, who was Japan's minister of foreign affairs from 1982 to 1986. Abe personalized that lineage in his "Alliance of Hope" address at a historic joint session of the US Congress in April 2015, when he spoke about how former enemies could become friends and allies, and of the lasting power of peace and reconciliation. Because Abe had stepped outside of traditional boundaries in advocating for Japan's international role, there was a huge controversy around celebrating his life, and at first it wasn't even certain that there would be a national funeral. What I found most interesting was the response by the bureaucracy and Japan as a nation. When a leader dies it is normal to celebrate their life and, in some ways, whether someone is killed or whether they die naturally, one considers only the positive. In the case of Abe, Japan needed to give itself permission to celebrate Abe's life, and that this took place is a testament to the long tradition of *gaiatsu* or outside pressure for change from beyond Japan. Usually this foreign pressure, especially from America, is perceived as a catalyst for domestic change that often involves external demands or expectations that prompt Japan to implement policies it might not otherwise pursue. Essentially, it's the idea that external pressure is needed to push Japan toward reforms or policy shifts. The most quintessential example is Commodore Perry's Black Ships in 1853 which opened Japan to the world or the post-World War II reforms that General MacArthur imposed, or even the trade negotiations of the 1980s that continue to resonate in the current global economic context. In the US, it took the Japanese Embassy and Consulate several days to figure out how to handle the outpouring of American support; the enormous number of people who showed up at the Consulate in New York to sign the condolence book there is a testament to Abe's strong connection to America that I also witnessed first-hand.

Prime Minister Abe singularly personified America's affection for Japan. This was especially evident in his "Alliance for Hope" speech where Abe stated the following:

> Proactive contribution to peace based on the principle of international cooperation should lead Japan along its road for the future. Problems we face include terrorism, infectious diseases, natural disasters, and climate change. The time has come for the US-Japan alliance to face up to and jointly tackle these challenges that are new. After all, our alliance has lasted more than a quarter of the entire history of the United States. It is an alliance that is sturdy, bound in trust and friendship, deep between us. No new concept should ever be necessary for the alliance that connects us, the biggest and the second biggest

> democratic powers in the free world, in working together. Always, it is an alliance that cherishes our shared values of the rule of law, respect for human rights, and freedom.

Now, fifteen years after "Alliance for Hope" and with the departure of Abe's singular voice, the US-Japan alliance is being challenged in dangerous and unprecedented ways.

JAPAN'S EXISTENTIAL CRISIS

With the triple disasters of 3.11 Japan experienced its own existential crisis and as a result, Japan's political parties were able to unify for the first time in a number of years. Although a lot of people think about Japan as a one-party system, there are actually many parties in Japan, and one of the reasons that the Liberal Democratic Party (LDP) has been so strong is that the other parties were not able to unify. Shortly before 3.11 the Democratic Party of Japan (DPJ) consolidated from all of its different root parts, coming together to win the election and defeat Prime Minister Abe. After the devastations of 3.11 and the ineptitude of the DPJ government, including a series of failures at all levels from the prime minister to TEPCO (Tokyo Electric Power Company), the Japanese people had had enough and brought back the LDP with the thinking that it couldn't be worse than the DPJ government. That's when Prime Minister Abe got his second chance, something that is very unusual in Japanese history. Abe created a space where he became the longest-serving prime minister in Japanese history after what was by all accounts, including his own, an unsuccessful first term.

During his more than seven years as prime minister, Abe solidified Japan's role in the world and won the opportunity for Japan to host the Tokyo Olympics. As a master of personal diplomacy Abe had a great relationship with Donald Trump, far better than with any other

American president. He had more meetings with Russian President Vladimir Putin than any other world leader as well as warm relations with other national leaders from German Chancellor Angela Merkel to Turkish President Recep Tayyip Erdoğan and Israeli Prime Minister Benjamin Netanyahu. This kind of personal diplomacy has really been the exception in Japan, with Abe joining the pantheon alongside prime ministers Koizumi, Nakasone, and Yoshida.

What has Japan learned from the political disaster of 3.11? Unfortunately, it seems that the LDP hasn't actually learned that much. But Abe did. He learned about the importance of resiliency, efficiency, and effective communications. While the LDP may have only been around for seventy years, Japan as a society has existed far longer. There may not be factional systems in the LDP anymore since Prime Minister Kishida abolished them, but in Japanese society there are still factional groups that matter. Japanese political leaders have connections to the imperial family, prominent merchants, and the different tea schools that matter. That's something that we don't have in America's very diverse society, where our divisions are much more overt. Because of the strength and efficiency of the institutions behind the ballot box in Japan the government has learned the lesson of being responsive to the people. Japan's responsiveness is often underestimated by outsiders. To an outsider, no matter what happens, the country is still being run by a group of men, but these men might be from different groups known only to insiders, and they might be family, or kin, or otherwise interconnected. However, everyone in Japan knows where their leaders stand and what they represent, for the present and for the future.

JAPAN'S NATIONAL IDENTITY

One of Japan's greatest strengths is also its weaknesses in the way it defines itself in terms of national identity. Asking a Japanese person what makes them Japanese gets a quizzical look. Driver's licenses don't have hair or eye colors because most everyone has the same at birth. There is a conformity that is hard to explain in a place as diverse as New York and that might make it difficult for people who want to appreciate Japan. And even the concept of what it has traditionally meant to be an American is now breaking down in our polarized society. In this current fraught international environment, my sense of optimism comes from the individual level but what ultimately grounds me is family, faith, and friends. When I go to Japan and see my own family, not just my blood family but those whom I consider family, I'm optimistic when I think about the next generation of Japanese and how they're learning about being global citizens. In every dark space there is also great optimism.

What gives Japan such great opportunity at this moment is that its own well-being as a nation is no longer dependent on being number one. Whereas, with America, if we're not number one, then what are we? Americans see this as losing, but actually, like Britain and many other nations and empires, we have had a unique role in our nearly 250-year history. It is time to pass the baton on to the next generation, which doesn't necessarily want to choose between the US and China, just like Japan. Let's think about how Japan, the most homogenous nation in the world, can figure out its global footprint by using its soft power in addition to drawing on its global communities in countries like Brazil, which has the largest Japanese diaspora. One of the reasons that Japan is so popular today is that it has an amazing culture that both insulates you and asks you to challenge your own ideas by looking inside yourself. The Zen philosophy of controlling what can be controlled internally and adjusting our minds for what happiness or fulfillment looks like beyond material possessions is like a superpower in a capitalist society. There are a lot of lessons and much optimism to be had from a timeless and ancient wisdom that continually fulfills us and makes us better as human beings, whether with a bowl of tea or mindful meditation. We all have a yearning to be part of something that is bigger than ourselves, which is why nations exist. In many ways, this book is being written as a guide to connect our national stories and narratives, to explain what motivates and drives Americans and Japanese through our own senses of *ikigai* and purpose.

BEYOND THE *GENKAN*, AGAIN

Too often, those unfamiliar with Japan experience it from a distance—from the sleek, efficient facade of airports, hotels, and corporate lobbies. But to step beyond the *genkan*—the threshold of entry—is to enter a culture that thrives in the quiet spaces, the unspoken understandings, and the rituals that seem small but contain the universe.

In fact, a Japanese bowl of tea, received with openness after entering through the *genkan* and prepared with sincerity is perhaps the best example of how to experience Japan. It is a bridge—between host and guest, between past and present, between self and something greater. This, perhaps more than any political summit or cultural gala I've attended over my decades of life in Japan and Japan Society, captures the essence of Japan for me. It's in the whispered whisk of *matcha*, the glint of afternoon light on a lacquered tray, the humble bow before and after—a reminder that true connection requires presence, patience, and heart.

A moment that lives within me more vividly than almost any other from my time at Japan Society is not from our largest gatherings at our Annual Dinner or from speeches by prime ministers or celebrities, nor from a summit or program event, but rather from the quiet preparation and sharing of a single bowl of tea. The particular moments I remember didn't take place in a tatami-matted tea house, or even in Japan, although I've had my fair share of tea in such august settings. But the moment that most lives with me is this: it was at the Cathedral of St. John the Divine in New York City. It was March 2025 on the occasion of a World Peace Prayer Tea Dedication Ceremony with Yūyūsai Sōshō, the fifteenth Generation Grand Master of Omotesenke, who is one of the most famous and revered tea masters in Japan. For centuries, an entire school of tea-making has evolved from Omotesenke's teachings which, literally translated, means "the front of the Sen family." Growing up in Hokkaido, I didn't go to a lot of tea ceremonies or have any sense of the three main tea schools of Urasenke, Omotesenke, and Mushakoiisenke that play such a key role in many people's lives. And even though I've subsequently taken part in many ceremonies with each tea school since becoming president of Japan Society, this one was different.

As I watched the tea master purify and clean the cup, and make ready the vessel and the water, I finally saw that the preparation of a bowl of tea is actually a very powerful spiritual journey. I thought about the early history of Japan and how the tea ceremony had allowed warlords and feudal families to come together in peace, creating a space where, even in the midst of battle, weapons could be put aside. The respect that is shown by serving a simple bowl of tea, something that's been done in Japan for close to 600 years, is a harbinger of the harmony and peace that we need to find in our lives today.

"A BOWL OF TEA"

On another occasion, this time in Kōya-san, one of the most sacred places in Japan, I knelt across from the host, a master of *chado* (The Way of Tea) and Buddhist priest, I realized I was entering a world where time slowed, intention mattered more than outcome, and presence was not a virtue but a requirement. To truly appreciate what

I experienced that day and back in New York City at the cathedral, one must understand that the Japanese tea ceremony is not merely a performance or cultural artifact—it is a living expression of Zen philosophy, a distillation of Japanese aesthetics and values into one fleeting, unforgettable encounter. Rooted in the Muromachi period (1336–1573) and elevated by the legendary Sen no Rikyū in the sixteenth century, the tea ceremony evolved from a display of status into a practice of humility and inner stillness. Rikyū's emphasis on the principles of *wabi* (austere beauty), *sabi* (the elegance of aging), and *ichi-go ichi-e* (one time, one meeting) transformed tea from a beverage into a spiritual ritual. It is, in the deepest sense, an invitation to become fully awake.

A PERSONAL RITUAL OF RETURN

I remember watching the host's every move as he folded and unfolded the silk *fukusa* cloth with graceful precision. Each gesture had a purpose. Nothing was rushed. Nothing was wasted. Even the placement of the bamboo whisk, the ladle, and the ceramic bowl seemed choreographed not for show, but for reverence. I have sat through countless ceremonies before—some formal, others casual—but something about this moment struck me at my core. I wasn't there as a guest of honor or as the president of an institution. I was simply a participant in an ancient, sacred act of hospitality.

When the tea was finally placed before me, I bowed gently, turned the bowl twice, as taught, and took a slow, considered sip. The tea was slightly bitter, the warmth grounding. But what stayed with me most was the silence between us—not empty, but full. In that quiet, I heard centuries of wisdom and devotion. I felt deeply Japanese, not in nationality, but in spirit and one with the host whose silence spoke volumes.

CHAPTER FIVE

AMERICA'S PLACE IN THE WORLD AND WITH JAPAN

Receiving tea on a tatami mat in a church in New York with a priest or at Kōya-san with the Buddhist abbot is a privilege few Americans have. Yet its simplicity in remembering something essential about being human encourages me daily to share my own journey with Japan that began almost from birth. I want others to know about this for the betterment of our world, especially given the state of American politics and our quest for meaning as our government pledges to put "America First."

US CYCLES

American politics are cyclical, with every election bringing a pendulum swing between the parties and increasingly the extremes. Over the past thirteen presidential elections, Americans have gone between our two parties eleven times. A two-term consecutive presidency is becoming an exception. As a result, Americans seem to swing between not our "better angels," as President Abraham Lincoln might have called them, but our inner demons. With this most recent election, what we have brought upon ourselves is President Trump. Donald Trump has a lot of grievances about the economy including America's free markets and lack of tariffs going back to the 1980s that directly impact the US-Japan relationship. His fascination with cars and steel has been the most notable. Although many of these grievances were dismissed in his first term because the facts and the realities did not add up, in his second term we see a different set of players and results. President Trump is the best showman we've ever seen in American politics, and he has been able to convince people that although the facts might not show it, he's got a more compelling story and narrative around which to lead.

GLOBAL IMPACT

Changes in the US are having a significant impact on the postwar world order and rules-based law. Usually when there is such major change it is in the aftermath of a world war. However, there are major factors at play now and we don't need a world war to experience the lessons of history. Unfortunately, that may not be the case for the average American. This is where I feel a sense of urgency, not just to explain what's happening to my Japanese friends and to ask them to have patience and give us the benefit of the doubt, but also to ask Americans to learn from our own history. We need to analyze the past 150 years in terms of practical lessons we can learn for our democracy and economies. Our relationship with Japan—a relationship that went from fascination of the outsider to literally fighting each other to death to realizing that we needed a true alliance—needs to evolve beyond security and hard power to the human dimension. Unfortunately, the 2020s make it look like we're going back to that pattern of transactions of the 1920s rather than a cycle of transformation post-World

War II or through the Meiji Restoration. No one wants to go through a world war again, because next time we probably won't survive it.

The US did not become a global power until after World War II, along with the other major victor in that war, the Soviet Union. What happened in America before then didn't necessarily affect the rest of the world because the US didn't have as big a stake in the global economy. After the war, America's economy was almost fifty percent of the world's GDP, a number that has now been declining precipitously. What America has been very successful at exporting is the American model, the American way, and the American Dream. Over the past eighty years, the US has become a beacon of international stability and global order. But with the rise of China, which runs on a very different type of communism from the former Soviet Union, a ruthlessly efficient strategic player has emerged with basically no separation between private and public state companies. Investors driving the Chinese economy in America have to figure out how deal with the democratic system and political process alongside a very innovative private sector.

AMERICA IN THE ASIAN CENTURY

In some ways, the American democratic system and the private sector are now at war with each other. Is it poetic justice that Elon Musk, a billionaire from South Africa and the inventor of everything from Starlink to SpaceX, was asked by the president of the US to help make America more efficient through his self-championed Department of Government Efficiency, or DOGE, and then they had a spectacular break up? Unfortunately, what DOGE unleashed and is doing on behalf of the current administration has seriously imperiled America's standing and role in the world by tearing down respected institutions like the Voice of America, USAID, the Wilson Center, and the US

Institute of Peace, among others, all of which have had strong Japanese divisions. These divisions were put in place to help enhance US-Japan relations during a number of different bipartisan presidencies, not just under John F. Kennedy or Ronald Reagan. What is not as obvious to the American people is that it is a lot easier to tear down institutions than it is to build them, because that requires an external force of some kind much like Japan's version of *gaiatsu*.

America is looking particularly weak now on the global scene, especially as a global power. In contrast, Japan seems to be working efficiently to deploy its global development assistance and trade policy along with its soft power ambassadors, from Hello Kitty to green tea, all without a strong prime minister or an offense-capable military force. I would never bet against America but I'm worried that America's own worst enemy is itself, in both a national and a global context. Populism is not unique to America, and there are certainly populists and autocrats all over the world. However, America in some ways is going to shape the next century. If this is the Asian Century, as many grand strategists, including Kishore Mahbubani, have written about, and America is looking at the Indo-Pacific from the point of view of security, then the US-Japan relationship must be an anchor of stability. If not, it will be the catalyst for a centrifugal force that will only cause more chaos.

When I think about optimism, I think about countries like Türkiye, India, or Brazil, where no matter what is happening between the US and China or the US and Russia, these nations are doggedly optimistic, despite their populist and sometimes authoritarian leanings. And they're optimistic because it's looking like it may be the Global South's moment on the global stage. America should also be optimistic, precisely because thriving immigrant populations are making this country better. That's the greatest strength of America, in my point of view.

COVID CONSEQUENCES

One major effect of the COVID pandemic was to greatly exacerbate the already rampant divisiveness present in American society. Five years after the pandemic, there is still much to unpack alongside the shifting political sands. The quality of American leaders' response to the crisis will ultimately be decided by recorded history. Take, for example, former New York Governor Andrew Cuomo, who was once seen as the personification of efficient government. Lauded for his work during the pandemic but then chased out of office in disgrace and then soundly defeated mayor of New York City, where the work Cuomo did during COVID became a political tool to bolster or criticize his candidacy.

In the beginning of the pandemic, everything was about communication. Government institutions themselves had been under attack for a while, something that had certainly accelerated during President Trump's first term. Five years ago, some people were dismissive and others were alarmed because they didn't trust the government to give them the right information. That's how Dr. Anthony Fauci became a flashpoint for the National Institute for Health, and why, before President Trump's return in 2025, he resigned, as he had become a political enemy because he wouldn't let science bend to political will. Masks, ubiquitous in Japan to protect neighbors from one's own illness, became a symbol of protecting oneself in America, and later, influenced by backward thinking, masks began to be associated with taking away someone's freedom and thereby being a bad citizen. It was all about fear on both sides of the fence, and this was in some ways a microcosm of the way that the COVID pandemic ultimately would play out in both the US and Japan.

COMMUNICATIONS

The communications factor is something that links all crises. First, there's the immediate news in the aftermath of the crisis. Then, there's how the government responds, including what they think about the crisis and how they present themselves to the media. All of this is meant to reassure the public that government leaders are standing together with the people. That can backfire, because if someone doesn't have the facts and isn't well educated, it can be difficult to communicate with them. At the beginning of the COVID pandemic, national leaders in both the US and Japan failed to meet the moment. Local leaders stepped up to pick up the slack, especially in New York, providing details that were not coming from the White House. During 3.11, the US Embassy, prefectures, mayors, town leaders, and nonprofit and civil leaders alike had to turn to different sources outside of the government or TEPCO to find the information that mattered. That information wasn't coming from the prime minister's office. At that time, social media was generally trusted to provide accurate information, something that is no longer true today when social media is a self-reinforcing bubble of whatever people want to hear and rampant disinformation that has not been verified and yet goes viral. This is a technological threat that we didn't have during the last crisis—and it is also a danger to democracy.

No discussion of crises, especially in New York, would be complete without 9/11. We all remember where we were on September 11, 2001. For me, 9/11 was a transformative moment that set me on my path to Türkiye and further down the road, to Japan Society. Even those who were not yet born at that time feel the impact of the 9/11 memorials. By reading the lists of victims and their nationalities, many of them Japanese, we remember that 9/11 wasn't just an attack on New York; it was an attack on the world. While that triggered a global war on terror and an invasion of Afghanistan, the deep wound in New York certainly had an impact on Japan.

GLOBAL REFORM

In a tumultuous world it is necessary to have hope—for peace, for understanding, and for reconciliation on both personal and societal levels. There are certainly reasons to be optimistic in terms of technological advances. There's also the fact that the United Nations has lasted nearly eighty years. Rather than complaining that the UN is impotent, let's think about how eighty years for the UN compares with the League of Nations, which lasted only twenty-six years. It is time to take reform at the UN seriously and include countries like Japan and Germany, which have been excluded from permanent seats on the Security Council because of their actions in World War II. Japan pays the third highest UN dues but has no ability to influence the final outcome of the Security Council, where ultimately China or Russia can veto everything. Japan and Germany need to be included, and the UN Security Council needs to be reframed around a more relevant metric for the twenty-first century, such as the G20, as it no longer matches the pragmatic realities of the world.

After the failure of the League of Nations, which President Woodrow Wilson conceived but the US ultimately didn't join, the lesson learned was to be pragmatic. The UN has great ideals such as the Universal Declaration of Human Rights. On a mechanical level the UN is doing incredible work for health and human services, and in helping refugees and acting as peacekeepers. Of course, there's also inefficiency at the UN, but the political consensus for a reset won't happen unless there is another world war. When the UN was created, the main players were acknowledged, but not all the main players are present now. Where is India, with the largest population in the world? Where is South America or Africa? It is obvious that Europe is completely over-represented. UN Security Council reform shouldn't be that complicated. If that's not changed, and no leader steps forward or even shows up to represent their country, we're going to have a hard time because no one expects the UN to solve world peace—but this is exactly where world peace would be debated.

NIPPON STEEL

While this book was being written, the Nippon Steel crisis—and it was a crisis of faith in the free market, not just an acquisition gone wrong during a tough presidential election—was ongoing, with detrimental impacts on US-Japan relations that included a lawsuit against former President Joe Biden and much handwringing by Japan, Inc., at Nippon Steel's perceived fumbling of the American way of doing business in an election year. First, let's talk about steel. Without steel almost nothing can be built. Throughout modern history, steel has become the one resource necessary for true hard power in both the economic and military sense. As Japan's iconic steel company, Nippon Steel is an important cultural phenomenon with a history predating World War II. *Nippon* means "Japan." This is very telling. The fact that it wanted to acquire US Steel is equally telling, because US Steel's name is also iconic in America, especially as its homebase is Pittsburgh. With the consolidation of steel companies, and competition from China, the only way for America's steel industry to survive was through major investment in high-precision and quality steel-making, for which Nippon Steel is known. The result was the historic acquisition that led to a bidding war toward the end of 2023, just before one of the most contentious presidential elections in American history. It was the worst possible timing for a surprise announcement of this type.

The extremely negative reaction that followed in the US was directed not only against Nippon Steel but also against Japan in general. It was as though Japan had tried to buy America in an underhanded way, coming out of left field. Most Japanese business transactions are not as opaque;

there is great transparency in Japanese business transactions. Most Americans don't know that Nippon Steel is in many ways as much an American company as it is a Japanese company, with already substantial investments in the US prior to the acquisition bid, including a Nippon Steel mill in Pennsylvania. The timing was tight because of competing bids, and Nippon Steel had to make a very quick offer when US Steel was put up for auction, bidding against Cleveland-Cliffs, an American company based in Ohio. After coming in second place, Cleveland-Cliffs began a full-blown PR attack campaign on Nippon Steel's credentials using 1980s Japan bashing tactics along with racist tropes. Leaning into the worst instincts from World War II and purposely demonizing Japanese as being worse than the Chinese despite being fellow democracies and the largest investors in the US economy, this campaign demonstrated the power of storytelling which the Japanese are unaccustomed to doing in a business context, since they believe quality speaks for itself. Especially in a political year like 2024, Democrats and Republications alike came out swinging to use the acquisition for their own political agendas. Most importantly, the CEO of the United Steelworkers union had not consulted his union members, so they were up for grabs political and up in arms. This, despite the fact that jobs and wages would benefit from the deal. But the union workers wanted more leverage. Additionally, Pennsylvania, the home of US Steel, became the ultimate swing state in the 2024 election. In Japan, most companies ran for cover from this public relations fiasco. Even Prime Minister Kishida was very cautious in his response, even though the acquisition was in Japan's national interest. It wasn't until Prime Minister Ishiba and President Trump were elected that economic interests prevailed.

ACTION AND REACTION

The Nippon Steel crisis illustrates the fragility of US-Japan relations. Years before, the deal would have been made in a smoke-filled backroom between the president, prime minister, and CEOs. But now, there are more actors involved in every decision. As we will see, that new reality has its pros and cons. The acquisition of US Steel was a rational and economically smart deal given the types of investment and technology the American steel plants needed and that Japan and Nippon Steel were best suited for. But, in politics, it is not always about rationality; often, it is about emotion and optics. In some ways, the deal was fraught from the start because the preparatory work—consulting with everyone who would be affected and proactively educating stakeholders, which should have been done by Nippon Steel decades before—just did not happen. If that had happened, it might have led to a different approach but the same outcome. President Biden rejected the acquisition using the Committee on Foreign Investment in the United States (CFIUS), a provision in American national security to block the sale of something that is of national security interest to an adversary of the United States, something that is generally meant to be used against Chinese investors. Japan had never been subjected to this type of scrutiny previously, but the US Steel acquisition became such a political hot potato that the president had to find a way to stop it. In fact, ultimately by choosing to sue former President Biden, Nippon Steel left the door open for President Trump to consummate the deal. He finally did with a "golden share" that guaranteed Washington's approval for any major changes or divestments.

As will be discussed in subsequent chapters, Japanese companies, including Toyota, have successfully navigated American politics and business partnerships before. But the fact that the US Steel acquisition became so fraught, while everyone in the US-Japan space was arguing the rationality of that deal, demonstrates the work that still needs to be done. It is true that Nippon Steel did not prepare itself well for the acquisition and that the CEO of US Steel in some ways did what was in his own best interests and did not consider his workers in the decision.

This follows a general trend in American business practices: Following President Trump's election to a second term, the divide between the American blue-collar working class and white-collar employees is now playing itself out in a spectacular fashion across our nation.

As a result, many Japanese companies have become concerned that investing in the US might not be as certain or fruitful as it has been in the past. That's not just because of upsets in the rule of law, it's because increasingly Americans cannot be rational when it comes to politics. In other words, something might make all the business sense in the world, but in the end, many Americans will default to a xenophobic position to stop the deal as was attempted in the US Steel case. Now that it is resolved, Americans and Japanese alike will be studying this case long into the future as a cautionary example of what Japanese companies should and should not do, with leadership the key point on the US side of the equation.

CHAPTER SIX

JAPAN IS ALREADY DEEPLY EMBEDDED INTO AMERICA

Long before the Nippon/US Steel case, in the 1980s, Toyota was the symbol of Japan's economic ascendancy—and, for many Americans, a scapegoat for its own economic insecurities. As US manufacturing declined and trade deficits widened, Japanese automakers, with their efficient production systems and fuel-efficient cars, became targets of frustration. It was a time when Congress held hearings accusing Japan of unfair trade practices; when Detroit unions blamed Toyota for lost jobs; and when anti-Japanese sentiment boiled over in acts of violence—most tragically in the 1982 murder of Vincent Chin in Detroit.

This era, known in policy circles as the "Japan bashing" years, served as a harsh but invaluable learning moment for Toyota. The company—already global in reach—came to understand that success in America required more than a good product and efficient logistics. It required political fluency, local legitimacy, and strategic empathy. Today, Toyota is not only the most successful Japanese automaker in the US, it is also widely regarded as having one of the most sophisticated and effective government affairs operations of any foreign company operating in America. That transformation—spanning four decades—is a case study in how corporate diplomacy, strategic localization, and long-term trust-building can turn cultural crisis into geopolitical capital.

THE SHOCK OF THE 1980S

In the 1980s, Toyota executives were blindsided by the intensity of a backlash. While they had focused on improving quality, expanding dealerships, and cutting costs through lean manufacturing, they had underestimated the political and emotional weight of their success. The company's cars were popular, but the company itself was foreign, unfamiliar, and—at times—viewed with suspicion. Back then, Toyota had limited political representation in Washington. Its US leadership was modest in size and largely deferential to headquarters in Japan. While Toyota engineers revolutionized global manufacturing through the Toyota Production System (TPS), their public affairs strategy lagged far behind. As Japan's trade surplus ballooned, Toyota and its peers were caught in the geopolitical crosshairs. Import quotas, tariffs, and congressional threats loomed much like today. Toyota knew it had to change, which lead to its pivot.

THE PIVOT

Toyota's initial response was economic localization. Beginning in 1984 with New United Motor Manufacturing, Inc. (NUMMI), a joint venture with General Motors in California, Toyota signaled its willingness to invest in American workers and communities. But the turning point came in 1986, when Toyota opened its wholly-owned manufacturing plant in Georgetown, Kentucky—the company's first major US assembly operation. This was more than a factory; it was a statement.

By building cars in America, employing Americans, and integrating into the local economy, Toyota changed the narrative. It was no longer an exporter invading the American market; it was an employer contributing to it.

Toyota's commitment didn't stop at assembly lines. It began to invest in community partnerships, workforce development, educational initiatives, and local philanthropy. Over time, Toyota transformed its US footprint from a commercial operation into a civic one.

BUILDING INFLUENCE THE AMERICAN WAY

By the 2000s, Toyota had learned that local factories and jobs were only part of the equation. To shape its operating environment—and protect its reputation—it needed a stronger voice in the corridors of power. Toyota built a top-tier government affairs team headquartered in Washington, DC, and embedded staff in state capitals where its manufacturing footprint was largest. It hired American experts in public policy, communications, and lobbying—many with prior experience in Congress or the executive branch. Toyota Motor North America (TMNA) became more autonomous and integrated into the US political landscape. The company also became one of the most active foreign-based corporate donors to US political causes and trade associations—carefully bipartisan in its approach. Toyota's engagement with the American Legislative Exchange Council (ALEC), the US Chamber of Commerce, and industry-specific lobbying groups reflected its pragmatic approach to policy influence.

Crucially, Toyota also built relationships across the aisle. From Republican governors in the South to Democratic members of Congress in industrial regions, Toyota framed itself not as a foreign firm, but as a local employer with global reach. Its executives made frequent visits to Washington, appeared at congressional hearings, and developed relationships with thinktanks and journalists. This paid off. During trade disputes, regulatory battles, and even the 2010 recall crisis—when Toyota faced unprecedented scrutiny over vehicle safety—the company's strong US relationships helped contain the fallout. Congressional allies defended Toyota's record and governors reminded the public of the thousands of jobs Toyota supported in their states. The company's long-cultivated local ties became a form of insurance.

IMPLICATIONS FOR THE US-JAPAN RELATIONSHIP

Toyota's evolution is not just a corporate success story; it has broader significance for US-Japan relations. In many ways, Toyota has done more than almost any other entity to humanize and localize the Japan-America partnership in the eyes of ordinary Americans. In Alabama, Kentucky, Indiana, and Texas, "Japan" is not an abstraction; it's an employer, a partner, and a neighbor. This embeddedness is a critical buffer in today's volatile political environment. As the federal government becomes less predictable and foreign policy becomes more erratic under populist administrations like Trump's, localized ties become even more important.

Toyota's grassroots and institutional presence in the US have helped Japan maintain its influence even during moments of bilateral tension. Other Japanese firms—Mitsubishi, Hitachi, Panasonic—have followed suit, but none as successfully or as early as Toyota. Toyota's journey from pariah to political powerhouse is a testament to adaptation, humility, and long-term thinking. By learning from the bitterness of the 1980s, Toyota has forged a durable model of corporate diplomacy that continues to serve both its interests and the broader alliance between Japan and the United States.

In an era where the federal center may no longer hold and power is increasingly distributed, Toyota has shown that influence flows not just from Washington, but from Georgetown, from Huntsville, and from Plano. Japan's future engagement with the United States will depend not just on ambassadors and treaties, but on factories, school programs, and local trust. Toyota knew this before most. And today, it is reaping the rewards of having never stopped learning.

DAIKIN—FROM OSAKA TO DAIKIN PARK

Daikin's century-long journey from Osaka to Texas reflects a deeper transformation in how Japanese firms see their global roles. Unlike the export-first models of the 1980s, today's global players—like Toyota and Daikin—understand that durable success in America requires cultural fluency, decentralized decision-making, and long-term community investment. Daikin's approach balances *monozukuri* (the Japanese philosophy of craftsmanship) with market responsiveness. The company empowers its American engineers, managers, and designers to tailor products to local needs while maintaining Japanese quality standards. That blend is increasingly rare—and increasingly valuable—in a world where supply chains are being reassessed and local resilience is prized.

On a hot summer evening in Houston, fans stream into a familiar ballpark under a new name: Daikin Park. Once called Minute Maid Park, home to the Houston Astros, it now bears the name of a Japanese company that, until recently, was barely a household name in America. But for those paying attention, this symbolic renaming marks more than a branding coup. It reflects the coming-of-age of Daikin Industries, Ltd. in the United States—an Osaka-based HVAC powerhouse with global ambitions and an American strategy that may well redefine how Japanese companies wield influence and build trust abroad.

From its massive manufacturing hub in Texas to innovation centers in Washington, DC, and a new presence in New York, Daikin is crafting a story that goes beyond market expansion. It's becoming a cultural and economic bridge between Japan and the US, harnessing America's love of baseball, climate-conscious innovation, and local investment to position itself as more than just the world's largest air-conditioning company—it wants to be America's HVAC company, too.

TEXAS-SIZED INVESTMENT

Daikin's ambitions in the American market are anchored in Daikin Texas Technology Park (DTTP)—a sprawling 4.2 million square-foot facility in Waller, Texas, just outside Houston. Completed in 2017 with an estimated $450 million investment, it is one of the largest HVAC manufacturing facilities in the world. It combines manufacturing, engineering, logistics, and office functions under one roof and employs thousands of American workers. The DTTP represents more than manufacturing scale; it's a symbol of localization done right. By producing directly in the US, Daikin has reduced costs, shortened supply chains, and improved responsiveness to American customers. Just as Toyota learned in the 1980s that long-term success in the US required American jobs and community investment, Daikin is proving that "Made in America" can be a Japanese strength.

Just as importantly, this facility has made Daikin a major economic player in Texas —one of the most dynamic growth regions in the country and a core base of political influence that Japanese companies like Daikin and Toyota are flocking to. In Texas, Daikin and Toyota are not foreign companies; they are local employers, job creators, and civic partners.

INNOVATION WITH A MISSION

Daikin's US strategy isn't limited to Texas or scale—it's about strategic presence. In 2024, the company opened its new Technology and

Innovation Center (TIC) in Washington, DC, aimed at aligning Daikin's cutting-edge, energy-efficient technologies with evolving American climate and energy policies at the heart of American power across the street from the White House. As the US increasingly shifts toward electrification, carbon reduction, and smart energy management, HVAC systems have become central to the conversation about building decarbonization. Daikin's advanced heat pump systems and next-generation refrigerants are not just products—they are policy solutions. And in Washington, where policy meets innovation, Daikin positioned itself across the street as an indispensable stakeholder in America's climate future.

Meanwhile, Daikin's new office in New York City opened in 2025, the media and finance capital of the US representing another critical step. It's a platform for branding, partnerships, and storytelling. With Japanese precision and American ambition, Daikin is learning to speak directly to American consumers, regulators, and thought leaders, not as a foreign supplier, but as a committed partner in the US market and society.

ENGINEERING THE FUTURE

Daikin's American story is still being written. But the early chapters point to something remarkable: a Japanese company that has learned from past trade tensions, understood the new rules of US engagement, and is now thriving by being both global and local. In the age of political polarization, climate urgency, and economic nationalism, Daikin's success offers a playbook not just for Japanese companies, but for the US-Japan relationship itself. It shows that trust is built through presence, performance, and people, not press releases.

From Osaka to Texas, from Washington to New York, Daikin is showing how infrastructure and innovation can become instruments of diplomacy. And in doing so, it is quietly becoming one of the most important bridges between Japan and the United States, not in theory, but in steel, circuit boards, and shared goals for a sustainable future.

A NEW STANDARD FOR JAPANESE COMPANIES

Toyota and Daikin's cases offer a blueprint for Japanese and other foreign companies seeking lasting influence in America. The lessons are clear:

- Don't rely solely on national governments: Companies must build direct relationships with US policymakers at every level—federal, state, and local.
- Localization must be cultural, not just logistical: Hiring locally, investing in communities, and empowering American leadership builds credibility.
- Engagement must be strategic, not reactive: Toyota and Daikin didn't wait for a crisis. They built relationships before they needed them.
- Stay politically neutral while investing in sports: By staying bipartisan, Toyota and Daikin have ensured their influence endures regardless of who controls Congress or the White House while they both have homes in Houston with the Rocket's Toyota Center and the Astro's Daikin Park.

Today, Toyota is often cited in Washington as the model of a foreign company that "gets it." It is not merely tolerated—it is respected. Daikin is increasingly defining its own model with climate innovation as a strategic bridge and cultural engagement.

SAKE AND *SENCHA* IN THE EMPIRE STATE

If you want to taste the future of US-Japan relations, you need only take a sip of sake or green tea—not from Tokyo or Kyoto, but from the Hudson Valley and Brooklyn. It's in these unlikely but inspired places that two of Japan's most revered brands—Dassai, the ultra-premium sake producer from Yamaguchi, and ITO EN, the global pioneer of unsweetened green tea—have each made bold bets on New York, not just as a market, but as a home, a base, and a message. And that message is simple: Japan and America aren't just allies—they are partners building a shared future, grounded in excellence, craftsmanship, and cultural pride.

BREWING DIPLOMACY, ONE GRAIN AT A TIME

Dassai, known for its polished and poetic *junmai daiginjo* sake, is a brand that has never been afraid to dream big. In 2023, it opened a state-of-the-art sake brewery and tasting room in Hyde Park, New York, just miles from both the FDR Library and Museum and the Culinary Institute of America. The symbolism is powerful. Here was a centuries-old Japanese tradition being transplanted—grain by grain, drop by drop—into American soil in the heart of the Hudson Valley.

Hiroshi Sakurai, Dassai's CEO, has often said that sake must evolve or die. But rather than dilute its essence, Dassai chose to preserve its purity by expanding its reach. Having been fired once by his father, as the third-generation proprietor Sakurai embarked on his self-described "crazy journey" to America, as he told us on the Japan Society stage in New York on May 17, 2025. The New York brewery uses rice from Arkansas, pristine Hudson Valley water, and Japanese technology and artisanship. It's a delicate fusion that honors both its heritage and its new home.

But Dassai's investment was never just about alcohol. It was about cultural trust that has paid off in spades. It's about the idea that a Japanese company can create the best sake in the world, not just in Japan—but in America—for everyone. That is soft power. That is diplomacy in a bottle that now appears everywhere in New York as far as the Empire State Building and Yankee Stadium.

ITO EN—A GREEN VISION

In a different New York City borough, Brooklyn, another Japanese institution has taken root—ITO EN, the company behind the iconic Oi Ocha brand, which has transformed green tea into a global lifestyle. When I first met Yosuke Honjo, the dynamic leader of ITO EN North America, he told me his dream was for Oi Ocha to become as recognizable in the US as Coca-Cola. At the time, I admired the ambition. Today, I see the strategy.

ITO EN has spent years building trust with American consumers—not by chasing fads, but by standing firm in its commitment to unsweetened, authentic Japanese tea. By sourcing from Japanese tea farmers while packaging and distributing in the US, ITO EN shows what a sustainable, ethical, and cross-cultural supply chain can look like. And their presence here isn't just about beverages. It's about creating a new cultural rhythm, where wellness, mindfulness, and heritage aren't niche, but mainstream. Since the COVID pandemic, green tea has come into its own moment in New York.

WHY NEW YORK?

The fact that both Dassai and ITO EN chose New York as their American launching pads is no coincidence. New York is more than a city—it's a stage. It is where ideas become global, where craft becomes culture. By investing in New York, Dassai and ITO EN are making more than sake and tea. They are making a statement: that the most powerful diplomacy today happens not in embassies, but in tasting rooms, cafés, and conversations. That to understand Japan, you must taste it. And that to build lasting alliances, you must build shared experiences.

In this way, both companies are writing a new chapter of US-Japan relations—one not defined by geopolitics, but by flavor, respect, and vision. In an age of disconnection, Dassai and ITO EN offer something profoundly human. They remind us that what we create together, we can share together. That craftsmanship can cross oceans. That hospitality can become diplomacy. And that a cup of green tea or a glass of sake can do more to bring two peoples together than a thousand policy memos.

QUIET "METHOD" POWER

While headlines often focus on military alliances, trade negotiations, or geopolitical flashpoints, some of the most profound forms of influence are subtle, long-term, and cultural. In the long story of US-Japan relations, two of the most quietly successful Japanese exports are not technologies or cars, but methods—educational systems that have changed how Americans learn: the Kumon Method for mathematics and reading, and the Suzuki Method for music, especially violin instruction.

Though they operate far from Capitol Hill or the geopolitical arena, Kumon and Suzuki have permeated thousands of American communities. They touch millions of American families. And they embody a deeply Japanese philosophy: that disciplined practice, steady progress, and respect for the child's capacity to grow can produce world-class results. In their success lies an underexplored opportunity for Japan: to leverage cultural capital and shared values as a foundation for a new era of grassroots influence in America.

THE KUMON METHOD

Kumon began in 1954 in Osaka, Japan, when high school math teacher Toru Kumon created worksheets to help his son master mathematics through daily practice. The core of the method is deceptively simple: short, incremental exercises completed daily, emphasizing mastery before progression. Kumon's genius lies not in revolutionary content, but in its rigorously structured learning arc—students progress based on ability, not age, and develop deep foundational fluency. Today, Kumon operates over 1,500 centers in the United States and serves more than four million students globally. In the US, Kumon is especially popular among immigrant families and middle-class households striving to supplement public education. In states from Texas to California to New Jersey, Kumon centers are a fixture of strip malls and after-school routines.

The impact is profound. Students who follow the method over years often outperform their peers, not just in math but in study habits and self-discipline. For American parents, Kumon is not a Japanese export—it's an integral part of their child's success story. More importantly, Kumon represents a "soft power" triumph: it quietly embeds Japanese values of incremental mastery, long-term discipline, and self-paced learning into the daily lives of American families. It is a trust-based system that fosters deep parental involvement—aligning perfectly with community-level engagement.

THE SUZUKI METHOD

In parallel, Dr. Shinichi Suzuki revolutionized music education by asking a profound question: What if we taught music the same way we teach language? Inspired by the natural way children learn their mother tongue, Suzuki developed a method rooted in listening, repetition, early immersion, and emotional connection between teacher, parent, and child. Introduced to the US in the 1960s and 1970s, the Suzuki Method flourished in a country searching for more holistic educational approaches. It emphasized not just technical skill but character development. Teachers were trained to encourage, parents became co-teachers, and children began learning violin—and later piano, cello, and flute—as young as three years old.

Today, Suzuki programs exist in every major city in the United States, embedded in both private music studios and public school systems. Suzuki-trained musicians fill the ranks of orchestras and conservatories across the country. And, like Kumon, Suzuki families form tight-knit communities centered on trust, excellence, and transnational connection. In Suzuki lies another core strength of Japanese influence: relationships before results. The method's emphasis on empathy, patience, and familial involvement has resonated across American cultural lines from urban centers to rural towns.

THE FUTURE IS ALREADY HERE

As Japan navigates a new American political environment shaped by decentralization, populism, and the erosion of federal norms, its path forward must be guided not only by alliances and treaties—but by relationships. Kumon and Suzuki are living proof that Japan can deeply shape American lives without coercion, transaction, or fanfare. They show that influence can be quiet, cumulative, and long-lasting. They offer a roadmap for engagement that is more resilient than any trade deal or summit handshake.

In a world of shifting geopolitics and cultural anxieties, the next chapter of US-Japan relations may depend less on military bases and more on math worksheets and violin lessons. Japan's best ambassadors may not be diplomats or CEOs, but teachers, students, and parents—building trust one note and one problem set at a time. These systems are not transactional, they are transformational. This grassroots credibility is what Japanese policymakers and business leaders must recognize and amplify. The quiet success of Kumon and Suzuki suggests that Japan's most enduring power in America may lie not in Washington, but in living rooms, after-school pickup lines, and music recitals.

PART TWO

GROWING UP BETWEEN JAPAN AND AMERICA

Learning to Become a Global Bridge-Builder

CHAPTER SEVEN

DOSANKO AND MY FAMILY'S CONNECTION TO JAPAN

My family history with Japan begins with my grandfathers, who both served in the Pacific during World War II. My maternal grandfather, Dr. Lewis Graham, was a B-29 bomber pilot and a flight instructor in the Air Force and my paternal grandfather, Carlton Walker, Sr., somewhat younger than Lewis Graham, was part of General Douglas MacArthur's Army Occupation forces, serving primarily in the southern island of Kyushu in the Beppu area. Dr. Graham, who became a dentist on the GI Bill, rarely spoke directly about his experiences during the war. He was in general a man of very few words and my grandmother talked enough for both of them every time I was around. Although he flew over Japan and took part in sorties, I don't think he ever set foot in the country until my family moved there when I was a year old.

Still, Dr. Graham had a deep connection with Japan because his service in the Air Force shaped him. One of my cousins once pointed out that Dr. Graham's service coincided with B-29s firebombing Tokyo and other major cities in Japan, including the atomic bombs that were dropped on Hiroshima and Nagasaki. When my paternal grandparents came to visit us in Japan, sometimes my grandmother would mention to everyone that Dr. Graham had served in World War II and that she was very proud of him. My grandfather, though, never talked about the war—especially in Japan, where there seemed to be an uncomfortable presence looming in the background with many family histories that were left unsaid. Growing up talking about the war always seemed off limits with Dr. Graham whereas it wasn't with my other grandfather, Carlton Walker.

Carlton Walker was the life of the party, a man of many words who would become a life insurance salesman after the end of his service. As family legend has it, he signed up for the Army before he was of legal age and had to use all of his persuasion to convince his mother to sign on his behalf. He was still in training and hadn't seen combat when he ended up in Japan right after the war. Walker's work in the Occupation forces was to go door to door and take weapons away—including samurai swords and other prohibited weapons. Yet there was no sadness since he seemingly had never seen combat and was just an Occupation soldier following orders. Decades later, he would comment when he visited Japan that those swords would be worth millions today.

Carlton Walker, Sr., always talked about his Occupation experiences—how nice the Japanese were and how much they appreciated the chocolates and cigarettes that he would give out. He could only remember two phrases in Japanese: *do itashimashite*, which he remembered by using the phrase "don't touch my mustache," and *mizu ima*, a very impolite way of asking for "water now," which always made him laugh hysterically when he used it in a restaurant and made me cringe imagining the startled reaction of the polite Japanese waiters. The memory of both of my grandfathers visiting me in Japan is something I cherish.

My most vivid and relevant memory comes from when I was nine or ten. Dr. Graham and I visited Tamaki-*ojisan* (grandfather), the father of a member of my parents' church who I considered to be like my Japanese grandfather. I was translating for both of them, since they didn't share a common language. Tamaki-*ojisan*, a short man who was casually dressed, was talking about his experience being a part of the fighting and the Japanese retreat in Okinawa and whatever other Pacific islands he had served on—how frightening the roar of the B-29s and Flying Fortresses were, and just how terrifying the war had been. Dr. Graham, who was very properly dressed and much taller than Tamaki-*ojisan*, didn't mention that he had been a B-29 pilot, he just sat in his chair and listened quietly while I interpreted. In the end, the two of them reached an understanding when Tamaki-*ojisan* hugged Dr. Graham, saying, "Thank you for defeating us"—meaning that the Japanese had needed to be rescued from themselves, that the fascist regime in Japan had gone too far and so he didn't bear any resentment.

This was my first moment of understanding that my grandfather might have done "bad things" to the Japanese people during the war—people I had grown up loving—and that there were deeply buried stories which could never be known or told. That's a pretty intense moment, even for a pastor's son and missionary kid who sometimes played the role of counselor and discussant in small groups well beyond my years, given that I had been disciplined at home to help others. At that young age I was both witness and interpreter for these two veterans who had fought on opposite sides, who might have killed each other but basically ended up thanking each other for their service.

"Thank you for defeating us" might sound paradoxical, even jarring, to those unfamiliar with the profound arc of postwar history between Japan and the United States. But beneath those words lies the essence of a transformation more powerful than any military victory: the reinvention of Japan through peace, democracy, and alliance. Central to this rebirth was the Yoshida Doctrine, named after Prime Minister Shigeru Yoshida, who led Japan during the critical years of its reconstruction after World War II. With Japan's cities in ruins and its military dismantled, Yoshida charted a pragmatic path focused on economic recovery, political stability, and alignment with the US as the guarantor of Japan's security. He accepted the US military presence on Japanese soil, not as a mark of defeat, but as a strategic choice to "embrace defeat" that allowed Japan to channel its national energies into economic growth rather than rearmament. In doing so, Japan avoided the burdens of militarization during the Cold War, prospered under American protection, and emerged as a democratic, pacifist nation anchored firmly in the Western liberal order. What Tamaki-*ojisan* meant in his gratitude to Dr. Graham was not a concession of subjugation, but an acknowledgment that the painful defeat of 1945 planted the seeds of a new beginning—one in which Japan rose from the ashes not with resentment, but with resolve, finding strength in partnership rather than in empire. The hug between my two grandfathers was more than personal; it embodied a historical reconciliation that reshaped Asia and anchored one of the most enduring alliances of the modern world that today is taken for granted and beginning to shift.

That legacy of reconciliation and renewal wasn't just something I studied in history books—it was the backdrop of my own life. I grew up in Hokkaido, Japan's northernmost island, where the quiet strength of the postwar generation and the deep cultural bonds between Japan and the United States were part of the air I breathed. From an early age, I straddled two worlds: the traditions and humility of my Japanese upbringing, and the openness and curiosity instilled by my American heritage. This lived experience—of seeing firsthand how two former enemies who were my family had became partners, how cultural understanding can emerge from shared purpose—shaped not only my worldview, but also my calling. It's what inspires me every day now in my role as president of Japan Society: to build bridges, foster dialogue, and ensure that the hard-earned peace and partnership our grandparents helped forge continue to flourish in the next generation.

DOSANKO

I call myself a *dosanko*, an American *dosanko* because I am an American who was raised in Sapporo, a city on Japan's northernmost island, Hokkaido. *Dosanko* isn't a Japanese term you often hear in the West. *Dosanko* is used mainly by people from Hokkaido to describe themselves, and it's a word that no foreigner ever uses because it is not taught formally; it's a colloquialism. You'd never use a term like *dosanko* unless you're talking about family members who are from Hokkaido. Technically speaking, to be a *dosanko* your grandfather and father must have been born in Hokkaido. In a formal sense, I don't count, although I lived in Hokkaido for seventeen years, because I was born in North Carolina and my father and his father were born in Virginia. Technically, if you look up *dosanko* in English you will find that it is a type of Hokkaido horse, but I use it as a term of identity and endearment to my heartland of Hokkaido. This designation allows me to signal to my Japanese friends my deep connection to Japan and my strong roots in Hokkaido even if I'm the first to admit that I wasn't born there. Who I am today has very much been shaped by where I grew up and my experiences there.

EARLY HISTORY

My parents are Southern Baptist missionaries with a deep commitment to their calling. My father, a pastor by training, was a student worker who often would coach soccer in Taiwan as a journeyman in a two-year missionary program and my mother was a nurse serving in the same two-year missionary program in Tanzania. They met, fell in love, and married, committing to going as a family to Asia, which my father was absolutely captivated by. As my mother did not want to return to Africa to raise a family, her only requirement was that they go somewhere that my father did not speak the language so that she would have an equal opportunity to learn with him. The two countries available to them at that time in East Asia were Japan and Taiwan, so the rest was history. I like to joke that they made the wrong choice from the point of view of missionary work; today, South Korea is almost half Christian and Taiwan is over five-percent Christian, while Japan is less than one percent.

I was born in North Carolina, and when I was one, my parents moved with me to Tokyo, where we stayed while they learned Japanese. Then they moved to Hokkaido, where we lived until I was eighteen. My first memories are of kindergarten. I went to a Japanese kindergarten, because, so I'm told, in Tokyo I had a Japanese babysitter and I learned to speak Japanese fairly quickly. My parents, who were learning Japanese for the first time, would get very frustrated that their two-year-old was babbling things in Japanese they couldn't understand.

After the Occupation ended in 1952, many Christian missionaries came from America to Japan to try to pick up the pieces after the war, creating new churches and really trying to proselytize. When my family moved to Japan in the early 1980s alongside the booming Japanese economy it was during the second missionary "boom," when American missionaries were making a concerted effort to become more a part of the culture. My parents could have gone to any part of Japan, but they chose Hokkaido, and their choice had a direct impact on me because they settled in the most remote area of Japan where there were very few foreigners living year-round.

Growing up in Hokkaido meant that I stood out everywhere I went—not just for how I looked, but for how I spoke, thought, and moved through the world. As an American child in a largely homogeneous society, I was constantly aware of being "the other," which was both isolating and formative. It forced me to learn the language quickly, adapt to customs deeply, and understand Japan not as an outsider looking in, but from within its cultural rhythms. That experience gave me a heightened sensitivity to identity, belonging, and the importance of empathy—skills that would later become central to my career and own identity. Being different in Hokkaido didn't just make me fluent in Japanese; it made me fluent in bridging worlds.

MISSIONARY KID

In 1982, the year I moved to Japan with my family, Japan was a very proud nation, excited about its economic success and filled with a strong sense of cultural superiority. Since the end of World War II, Japan had achieved economic success through a combination of government-led industrial policy, a strong work ethic, technological innovation, and close cooperation between bureaucrats, big business, and banks—culminating in the 1980s when Japan became the world's second-largest economy. There was a divide between the generations who had seen and experienced the horrors of war and those who had only known the "economic miracle." This miracle's roots go back to the postwar period, when the Japanese government—particularly through the Ministry of International Trade and Industry (MITI)—guided industrial policy, invested in infrastructure, and promoted export-led growth. Japan benefited from American security guarantees, access to US markets, and Cold War-era support, allowing it to focus on rebuilding and innovating. The election of Prime Minister Yasuhiro Nakasone and his personal relationship with President

Ronald Reagan ensured strong US-Japan cooperation—resulting in US military forces spreading out across Japan and throughout the Western Pacific in response to aggression by the Soviet Union. By the time Nakasone and Reagan forged their strong political and strategic alliance, Japan had already become an economic powerhouse, with the 1980s serving as a peak of that long-developed growth.

By the mid to late 1980s the Japanese way of doing business was seen as a model for the world. The Japanese way of doing business is often characterized by a deep emphasis on long-term relationships, consensus-building, and group harmony, or *wa*, rather than short-term profits or individual gain.

Unlike those living in expatriate communities such as military bases or the Tokyo area where there were already many foreigners, I had no choice growing up but to become a part of the fabric of Hokkaido. In general, missionaries tend to try to become part of the communities they serve. When my parents arrived in Sapporo, they were working with Annie Hoover, who I came to consider like my grandmother in Japan. A missionary from Arkansas who attended the same home church as Bill Clinton, she was one of the first Americans to arrive in Hokkaido after the end of World War II. Annie took us under her wing at Sapporo Baptist Church, where my father started as a missionary associated with the church who was asked to preach from time to time but was not technically a pastor, given the requirements of the time, and would go on to plant other churches in the city. He was a youth minister by training, and would preach periodically, but both my parents were still learning to speak Japanese fluently at that time.

I went to the Japanese *yochien*, or preschool, connected to my parents' church. There, I had the pressure of always being watched, especially since I was the only American kid in church where my mother was playing the piano and my father was preaching. Church is not a very kid-friendly environment for a four-year-old and I had a tendency to be loud and occasionally interrupt services. I felt that all eyes were on me, not necessarily because I was American, but because I was the pastor's kid. I was put on a pedestal and naturally I rebelled. There was a lot to live up to from a very early age because I was a foreigner—a *gaijin*—and a missionary kid and the son of the pastor.

HOKKAIDO INTERNATIONAL SCHOOL

As a student at the Hokkaido International School, which had only about a hundred kids from K–12, my best friends were Russian, Mexican, Japanese, and Lithuanian in a recording-setting class of thirteen with only two other American guys. I'd always stood out as an American, but at the age of sixteen I had a major growth spurt that made me stand out as a giant when walking onto subways. Playing basketball was the one place that I could channel my height and my outsider status, because being an American in Japan meant you had to be good at basketball. My basketball team was like a mini-United Nations—our starting lineup had Americans, Japanese, a South African, and a Russian. We played tournaments not only against local Japanese schools but the schools at American military bases, the closest of which was the Air Force base in Misawa, as well as traveling further south and even abroad to South Korea and the Philippines. As an American visiting a US military base I was filled with pride to see the power of my country in the flags flying everywhere and the way that the soldiers presented themselves. My understanding of the Japanese Self-Defense Forces was mainly based on the snow sculptures and ice slides that they made for the children each winter in Hokkaido.

My positive associations with American military bases continued until I encountered the darker side of that culture on the basketball court. Kids seemed to enjoy fighting more than sportsmanship. They used curse words rather than encouraging ones, which I was taught to do on my team and with my family. Coupled with my first encounter with the sleezier red-light-district elements overtly on display all around the base, I realized not all Americans in Japan were growing up like me. Rather than the idealized best-of-both-worlds I thought I had, these kids were living in a caricature of America that I did not recognize. I made a conscious choice not to be like those Americans but also not to be like those Japanese, and to somehow find a middle ground. I remember looking up to the base commander who would come to open all of our basketball tournaments and thinking that, one day, I'd like to speak with his conviction. In the same way, I saw the Japanese officials from the base community who introduced our tournaments as role models. I wanted to be part of both of these communities—not a representative of either, but in my unique space as both an outsider and an insider.

CHAPTER EIGHT

COMING BACK TO JAPAN

I decided to return to the US for college because I saw possibility and opportunity in America beyond Japan's highly structured higher education system. I realized that my life was going to be defined by my being an American and that no matter how much I felt like a *dosanko* on the inside, I would never be a Japanese national. I applied to American universities a few hours from where my grandparents were living in Virginia. I knew that I would not have my immediate family with me because my parents had made a commitment to their work in Japan. I chose to attend the University of Richmond, a private university set on an idyllic campus near where my grandparents lived. The school granted me a full scholarship.

CULTURE SHOCK

Richmond was a real culture shock. Even though I'd grown up in Japan, no one could tell it just by looking at me. In a place where the first question people asked each other was, "Where are you from?", I'd get a lot of odd reactions when I said I was from Japan. Although I thrived on being different and I liked shocking people by saying I was from Japan, that's not what they wanted. They wanted a comfortable conversation, something that was simple and easy and able to fit in a box. I've never been able to do that, despite looking like the quintessential American. Most people on campus looked like me, but I didn't feel like anybody else. Ultimately, I gravitated toward the international community and the African Americans and other minorities on campus. At that time, I wanted to be a pastor and I was actively involved in the InterVarsity Christian Fellowship. One of the things I did was to go to church in the inner city in Richmond where there was a large minority community. Despite being part of the "majority," I felt more comfortable in this community, probably given my own upbringing as a minority in Japan.

I discovered other things about being an American, specifically a Southern American, that were far less comfortable than what I'd learned in Japan. I didn't know that in Richmond the American Civil War was taught as the War of Northern Aggression, and that my family had fought on the Confederate side. It was a difficult and painful time to try to learn about my own history and family legacy that, unlike the case of Japan, was more complicated. My America-Japan story was easier to understand—the Japanese appreciated that both my grandparents had served in World War II and acknowledged that this had been a necessary evil for stopping fascism in Japan. In Virginia there was a much more complicated and nuanced history to confront as I learned what it meant to be an American all over again.

A YEAR ABROAD, WITH 9/11

What first sparked my interest in international relations was the tension I felt growing up between two cultures—Japanese and American—

and my desire to understand how nations, like people, navigate difference, conflict, and cooperation. I wanted to make sense of the world I was living in—a world shaped shaped by war and peace, identity and diplomacy, history and hope. As a result, in 2001, for my junior year, I wanted to go someplace outside of America and Japan to further expand my horizons. I decided on Europe. There was a choice of programs—peace and conflict at Uppsala University in Sweden, a similar program in Britain, and a program in Holland on European Union integration. I chose Leiden University in the Netherlands because it was the most historic university and was most centrally located so that I could travel extensively on the weekends. My goal at that time was to learn as much as I could about the European Union—how and why all these countries had come together after being so fiercely protective of their own sovereignties before World War II.

I got more than I bargained for. While the world watched the horror of 9/11 unfold, I experienced something very different—an act of unexpected kindness that changed my life. I was a twenty-year-old exchange student in Holland, but on that fateful day, my friend Jordan and I had traveled to Morocco, unaware of the chaos about to erupt. When the Twin Towers fell, we found ourselves in a tense crowd in Casablanca, suddenly vulnerable as Americans—and, in Jordan's case, as a Jew. Fear gave way to refuge when two Moroccan men, Mohammed and Abraham, took us in and welcomed us into their home. Over shared meals of couscous and broken conversations in French, Arabic, and hand gestures, we debated religion, history, and peace—a Christian, a Jew, and two Muslims trying to make sense of the unthinkable. While much of the world encountered the violence of Islamic extremism that day, I encountered the warmth of Muslim hospitality. That contrast deeply affected me. It sparked a desire to understand why such hatred could exist alongside such generosity, and it began my lifelong journey to engage with the Muslim world, to question assumptions, and to see America through the eyes of others. For the first time, I truly felt like a global citizen—shaped by my outsider status in Japan, but awakened by the events of a single, unforgettable week in Morocco.

FULBRIGHT FELLOW

When I returned to college for my senior year, the University of Richmond suggested that I apply for a Fulbright Fellowship. I had originally wanted to study in Greece because it was the birthplace of democracy, but because Greece was such a popular Fulbright destination my dean suggested that I focus on Türkiye. In my application essay I wrote about being a European American who had grown up in Asia and had a sympathy for Türkiye and the genius of its leaders. Initially my essay seemed aspirational, but Türkiye has since become a part of my personal history. Just like the Turks on their constant journey to the West, I was on a journey to discover who I was as an American. After the US invaded Afghanistan in response to the 9/11 attacks, Türkiye was among the countries that sent troops in support of US forces. It was Türkiye's unconditional support for the US that put me on the path toward applying there for my Fulbright, leading to another turning point in my life, one which also involved personal diplomacy and international relations.

My early interest in international relations deepened during my time as a Fulbright Fellow in Türkiye, where I served as a teaching assistant to Dr. Hüseyin Bağcı, a renowned professor of international relations at the Middle East Technical University in Ankara. It was a moment of heightened anti-American sentiment due to the US invasion of Iraq, yet I found myself welcomed and challenged in equal measure. The Fulbright program, run through the US Embassy, treated Fellows as cultural ambassadors—people tasked not only with academic work, but with representing their country through daily interactions. I embraced that role, speaking Turkish fluently thanks to its structural similarity to Japanese, and often surprising locals who had never met an American who could converse in Turkish. One unexpected relationship that came from this experience was with Ambassador Eric Edelman himself, whom I met not through formal diplomacy, but at a water park while joking around with his kids. That chance meeting led to a mentorship and showed me that cultural diplomacy is just as much about authentic human connection as it is about policy.

PRESIDENT BUSH IN TÜRKIYE

It was a pivotal moment for US diplomacy in Türkiye. In March 2003, under President George W. Bush, the United States had invaded Iraq. The intention was to destroy supposed Iraqi weapons of mass destruction and overthrow the regime of Saddam Hussein, who the administration had sought to link to the 9/11 terrorist attacks. Türkiye had just elected a new prime minister with very strong views on what is called Neo-Ottomanism—that Türkiye's role in the world was predicated on having been the former leader of the Muslim world and seat of the caliphate. In line with its new leadership, Türkiye's Justice and Development Party (AKP), its largest political party, voted to deny American forces access through Türkiye to the adjacent Kurdish region of northern Iraq. Going against Türkiye's express wishes, the US did what it wanted to, making President Bush one of the most hated US presidents in Turkish history.

By 2004, the Turks had managed to find a face-saving way of smoothing things over and Türkiye had become a key coalition partner for the US. It was the only Muslim majority nation of NATO and it had the second largest and most efficient group of soldiers in Afghanistan. Things had not been going well in Iraq and America needed

Türkiye's support. In advance of the NATO summit in Istanbul, President Bush was to arrive in Ankara at midnight for a high stakes meeting with Prime Minister Erdoğan and President Abdullah Gül. The hope was to bring the Turks back into a position of supporting the US efforts in Iraq and to get Türkiye to be one of the most important NATO players, because if America and Türkiye went into the summit unified, it was believed that all the efforts in both Afghanistan and Iraq would go better. Having lived in Türkiye for a year, I not only spoke the language but I also knew many of the main players. Once again, I found myself at the right place at the right time.

PRESS CORPS

I was asked to help with the press corps because I spoke Turkish, and I ended up being the main liaison on their bus, dealing with the press from America who were very cranky and very anti-Bush. Things didn't improve after a bomb threat at the Sheraton meant that no one got any sleep plus some people also had food poisoning. In the morning, after a short bus ride to the Çankaya Mansion, I was left to wait outside the secure meeting facilities with the exhausted and irritated press corps who couldn't seem to get enough of the mass protests. Demonstrators held up signs declaring death to America and depicting George Bush as Satan. The press bus had a big American flag on its side, and unlike the president's motorcade which was well protected by the police, we were very visible to the protestors.

After the meeting ended, the press and I boarded the bus that would take them to the airport where they would catch their plane to Istanbul to cover the NATO summit. President Bush's team went on the highway route, but there was some confusion because of all the protests. Our driver didn't speak English but my job was not to tell the driver what to do. However, the person from the embassy who was supposed to have been there was absent and I was on my own. I was busy providing the press with Turkish history and statistics that they had requested when I realized that we had become separated from the main motorcade and were now driving through the center of Ankara to Kızılay, the equivalent of Times Square in New York City. I knew that there was going to be a big anti-Bush, anti-America, and anti-NATO protest taking place there at noon. And it was going to happen while fifty Americans were driving through in a bus with a big American flag on it.

As we approached a sea of protesters. I started talking to the driver in Turkish. It turned out that he wasn't local and had no idea where he was going—he was just following the signs to the airport, not realizing that there was a checkpoint set up to go around the highway, which was out of the way but was the more secure route. I called the embassy on my phone, and they freaked out at the possibility of fifty members of the American press being accosted by protestors.

I told the bus driver to pull over by a taxi stand. I knew that Turkish taxi drivers, who are usually from the southeastern part of Türkiye, are known for their strong religion and tough attitude. As I got out, people began running towards us throwing rocks. I begged the taxi stand owner for help, saying that there were fifty American guests in the bus and that it would be really bad for him if anything happened to us. I appealed to his sense of manhood and also to the Turkish sense of hospitality, because in Türkiye the most important thing is being hospitable. Even if you despise your guests, if you are an honored guest, you must be taken care of. He gave me an indecipherable look, then grunted instructions to his cab drivers. We both jumped in the bus, where he yelled commands at the driver and the taxis, saying that if they didn't listen we were all going to be in big trouble. We drove behind ten yellow taxis that took the first part of the flank as we pushed through a huge mass of people who were literally shaking the bus. In this way we were able to leave the main downtown region through side streets where ordinarily a bus wouldn't go and finally reached the highway to the airport.

We arrived at the airport an hour behind schedule, but still with plenty of time to spare, as it turned out that the president had also been delayed by threats on the secure route. I'd lost communication with the embassy during the melee and the deputy press secretary of the White House was waiting for us at the airport with a look of pure panic on his face. He'd been in touch with the embassy and wanted to know what had happened. I said, "Well, we got out of there." It turned out that the press had been so busy filing their stories that they hadn't even noticed the danger that we were in. When they saw the deputy press secretary they started shouting questions, but he pulled me aside and said that he wanted me to know that the president personally thanked me for what I had done, and that this was something we needed to keep between ourselves. Then he gave me a set of cufflinks with George W. Bush's signature, saying that I had done a great service for the president. I still have those special cufflinks, which are very nice but which, I later learned, you can also buy in the White House gift shop. For me, this whole fiasco was a confirmation that people matter, that it can take a village (sometimes of taxi drivers) to get out of a really bad situation, and that I was truly appreciated by the people who make up the soul of the country. Each of us has a role to play, and at that time I was able to make a real contribution through people-to-people diplomacy and my knowledge and appreciation of Turkish culture. It was a validation of the way that human interaction can make a difference, something that I keep with me today.

INTERNATIONAL RELATIONS—YALE

Although I had already been accepted to the Sanford School of Public Policy at Duke University, Ambassador Edelman strongly recommended that I go to Yale for my master's in international relations, as that would be the best place to study grand strategy and diplomatic history with luminaries such as Paul Kennedy, Charles Hill, and John Gaddis. Plus, it was Edelman's alma mater.

At Yale, I realized how little most people knew about Türkiye. Scholarship on Europe and the Middle East was basically dominated by British, French, and German historians, with additional academic work on the Middle East by Persians, Arabs, and Israelis. Türkiye doesn't fit nicely into that bucket because its identity has always straddled East and West. It's an insider and an outsider in both areas, and it's home to the Muslim world's largest army. I found Türkiye fascinating from my study-abroad year and post-9/11 view of the world I had learned from my time in Holland and Morocco. Türkiye has long wanted to be part of the European Union. It is a Muslim democracy that has better opportunities to bring people together, whether in Iraq or Afghanistan, because—and this is particular to the Muslim world—there's a grudging respect for the Ottomans.

The more I learned at Yale, the more convinced I became there was something truly unique to explore through Türkiye, which I focused on almost exclusively during this time. Meanwhile, I continued to work for the State Department. Ambassador Edelman moved to the Pentagon as under secretary of defense for policy with Donald Rumsfeld, and I went to the State Department to serve on the Türkiye Desk, although I was really just a glorified intern with a graduate fellowship. Many career Foreign Service officers had resigned in protest after the start of the Iraq War, so I ended up running the Türkiye Desk almost like I was a Foreign Service Officer. Visitors would assume that I was an intern and ask me to make them coffee or tea, and when I went back to my desk they would be shocked that someone of my age was the Türkiye Desk person they were there to see. This taught me a lot about diplomacy and about how much speaking another language and understanding a different culture can change the dynamic. I also accompanied Turkish visitors to Congress and the Senate, where I learned a great deal about diplomacy and protocol. It was a very important time in US foreign policy. Türkiye's role in that era cannot be understated because of both its geography and its status as the former leader of the Muslim world, equivalent to the Vatican in the Catholic world. Additionally, I happened to know the main players in Türkiye's new government.

During my Fulbright in Türkiye, the foreign minister was one of the professors who took me under his wing, along with my main advisor at Middle East Technical University. I also became friends with the nephew of the president and the son of the prime minister. In fact, I knew most of the families and new political leaders, including Recep Tayyip Erdoğan in Türkiye's AKP. Few people in the US government were familiar with them because they had all been focused on the generals and the military who made up the traditional Kemalist secular elite. All of this became a really interesting case study in personal bridge-building and diplomacy for my career.

INTERNATIONAL RELATIONS—PRINCETON

My interest in Türkiye opened my eyes to the complexities of East-West identity, religion, and geopolitics. But over time, I began to see echoes of those same dynamics in Japan, the country where I grew up. The more I explored the Turkish desire to bridge civilizations, the more I was drawn back to Japan's own postwar journey of reinvention and its unique role as a cultural and strategic bridge between the West and Asia. What began as a detour through the Middle East ultimately brought me full circle, deepening my appreciation for Japan's global relevance and reigniting my passion to help tell its story to the world. I decided to pursue this curiosity through a PhD.

For my PhD, I decided to go to Princeton, which had the top program in international relations. At Princeton I worked with a lot of wonderful professors as well as area studies people who concentrated on East Asia, Europe, and the Middle East. I also organized a number of conferences, using my connections in the government to bring important speakers to the campus, something that very few people had done before. My academic research and intensity of focus on Türkiye's own national identify actually brought me back to Japan in a natural way, because I kept finding similarities between the experiences of Ottoman Türkiye and Japanese history. The crucial question for both nations was what it means to be an empire. Japan is often considered to be a late-developing empire because it only began to colonize and define itself as an imperial power in the late-eighteenth century. And its coming-out party only took place during the Sino-Japanese and Russo-Japanese Wars during the late-nineteenth and early-twentieth centuries. Japan's late development as a world power can be attributed mainly to the constraints of its external environment, as China and the Europeans were already very strong neighboring presences.

I wanted to put Japan's unique journey in a comparative focus with Türkiye. Looking at the history of these two countries and empires, I found that they're the opposite of each other. The Ottoman Empire started out in the fourteenth century as the preeminent power of its time. Its power reached its apex in 1452, when the Ottomans took over Constantinople. But by the nineteenth century, the Ottoman Empire was the sick man of Europe, a sort of rump state. Türkiye ultimately became a modern nation only because of its modern leader, Mustafa Kemal Atatürk, who leveraged the country's location as a crossroads of civilization and bridge between East and West, Europe and Asia.

In a similar way, Japan's geography has long shaped its identity. Because of its isolation as an island nation, Japan for a long time sought to remain apart from international entanglements. Surrounded by sea, Japan developed a sense of insularity and self-reliance. Japanese often interpreted its geography as a form of divine protection. This belief was crystallized in the idea of the *kamikaze*, or "divine wind." The divine wind became physically manifest in the thirteenth century, when sudden typhoons destroyed Mongol fleets and saved Japan from invasion. Over time, this reinforced a worldview that saw Japan as shielded by nature and destiny—able to selectively engage with the outside world on its own terms. This external environment, both physically isolating and spiritually affirming, shaped a foreign policy marked by caution, control, and a deep sense of historical continuity.

By the nineteenth century, the Japanese had to make their own destiny, and so they went to war to perpetuate their empire. That modern empire was ended by the atomic bombings of Hiroshima and Nagasaki and the termination of the Pacific War. It is fascinating that in the cases of both Türkiye and Japan, the US not only put an end to these empires but also generated security alliances that still stand today. Although the Ottoman Empire was defeated by the British Empire, the United States was included in the victorious Western powers that divvied up the country through the League of Nations. The reason that Türkiye became a member of NATO when it couldn't join the European Union is because of its geographic and strategic importance to the United States. Japan also rejoined the world community after World War II, becoming a key ally to America through the burgeoning US-Japan strategic partnership.

RETURN TO JAPAN

As I became more involved in studying Japan, I returned to Tokyo to stay with my parents, who were living there at that time, and I studied and taught at Tokyo University's beautiful Hongō campus. The more

I taught, the more I wanted to make it clear to my students that even though I grew up in Japan, I was not an expert on Japan—I was an expert on Türkiye. And yet the more I researched and talked about international relations, I would find myself using examples from both Japan and Türkiye, drawing naturally on my foundational knowledge of Japan. At that time, US-Türkiye relations were not going well, with Turkish democracy under assault and internal problems in the country that made it problematic for me to write candidly about Türkiye. And so, Japan became my main outlet and I returned to the government as an International Affairs Fellow at the Council on Foreign Relations and held various other research positions that had me interacting across the spectrum of the DC policy worlds.

3.11

On March 11, 2011, I was on vacation from my job in the State Department to celebrate my thirtieth birthday in Florida with my brother and friends when I watched the first news reports of the Great East Japan Earthquake, tsunami, and nuclear disaster. I knew the Tōhoku region well, because my parents had recently moved from Hokkaido further south to the main island of Honshu. The way the news was reported, it sounded like anyone who had been in the vicinity was dead. An even bigger nightmare was the meltdown at the TEPCO's nuclear reactor in Fukushima, where all Americans were being asked to evacuate. The cellphone network was down and I could not reach my parents. In that moment, when I thought I had lost my mother and father, I was reminded of how much I loved not just them but my heartland of Japan. I had taken Japan for granted because I'd been focused on Türkiye for almost ten years at this point since studying abroad in Leiden and my post-9/11 experiences. Watching the devastation of a country that I loved brought me home in many ways. What spoke to me the most was that the US had just experienced Hurricane Katrina a few years earlier, and the devastation in New Orleans wasn't just at the hand of nature, it was also at the hands of the American citizens who exploited the disaster. In Japan, it was the complete opposite, with everyone responding to the crisis in a most admirable way.

With 3.11, Japan showed its best, unlike the US during Katrina or with earthquakes in Türkiye. The fact that America was the first country to support Japan with its military forces after the triple disaster made me incredibly proud to be an American. I could see just how much our support at Japan's moment of need led to the Japanese opening up a little bit. What's interesting is that Japanese don't like to ask for help. In fact, it's considered rather rude in Japan to ask for help for anything, especially directly. But in that moment, the Japanese were surprised by the world's response, even though they couldn't understand why people really wanted to help them. Japan Society is a perfect example. After 3.11, starting with the very next day in the United States, Japan Society's Earthquake Relief Fund (JERF) raised more money for the disaster in Japan from private sector sources than from any other group. More than 24,600 donors from all fifty states in the United States and fifty-five countries around the world raised over $14.1 million, the seventh largest amount ever raised by the US nonprofit sector, with donations supporting more than forty-five organizations and sixty-five projects.

A few days after March 11, I was able to reach my parents. The first thing they said was not that they were safe, but that they were heading to the front lines in Sendai, working with the church community and the Tōhoku region to mobilize help. When I asked them why they hadn't called me, they said that they hadn't thought to let me know they were safe because they were more concerned about their community. It was powerful to see that their own personal calling to Japan had overruled their sense of well-being. That made me want to do more myself. As I watched the news coverage and spoke with my own policy community, I realized that the Japan policy world is very small and somewhat isolated in Washington, DC, even compared to Türkiye's presence. Also, my own personal connection to Japan trumped my policy expertise on Türkiye. This moment was about Japan, the second largest economy in the world at that time and one of America's most important allies. I wanted to understand and research more about the TEPCO disaster. Together with amazing stories of personal resilience, there had been a system-wide failure that included the government at the time, the prime minister, and TEPCO's leadership. All of this became something I could focus on academically, and I began to write about Japan again. The 3.11 triple disaster had reawakened and reaffirmed my service to US-Japan.

REENGAGING WITH MY HEARTLAND

I had taken my family, home and heartland for granted until I thought I had lost them in the devastating triple disasters of March 11. As I lived vicariously through my parents' relief work in Tōhoku, I was filled with pride for what they and America as a whole did for Japan in its moment of need. The word for friend, *tomodachi,* became ubiquitous at this moment in US-Japan relations as it was used by the US Embassy in Tokyo as a term for the relief projects spearheaded by Ambassador John Roos. As Kanji Yamanouchi, the first ambassador and consul general in New York with whom I worked as president of Japan Society, has reminded me, a friend in need is a friend indeed. My heart broke for the people of Japan—at how poorly understood and underappreciated they were in the world as their own sense of self failed to be reflected in the story of Japan's heroic recovery efforts. It wasn't the government's or TEPCO's responses that saved Japan, it was that Japanese society came together on its own, despite the lack of leadership. This was something I wanted to understand better and also celebrate. My role as a bridge-builder between Japan and the US had been reignited.

Now Japan was everywhere and I was uniquely suited to help through my language, family, and heart connections. Japan was a natural pivot point for me just like President Obama's foreign policy pronouncements towards Asia at that time. Using my academic training and experiences I began to seek out opportunities to engage with my heartland on a professional level, so setting myself on a new course. This, in turn, coincided with the reopening of Japan after 3.11 and the return of Prime Minister Abe to the political scene that would chart the course for Japan's global engagement, taking me from Asia Minor back to Far East Asia and my heartland of Japan. It was time to explore my true calling, or *ikigai,* which appropriately brought me back to my roots of connecting America and Japan.

CHAPTER NINE

THE INSIDE EDGE—REDISCOVERING MY *IKIGAI*

By necessity, all leaders have to be insiders. To lead effectively, one must understand not only the systems and structures of power, but also the cultural rhythms, shared values, and quiet assumptions that shape a society from within. Having grown up in Japan, I've come to appreciate that true leadership doesn't just move nations forward—it draws from deep wells of cultural continuity. Two concepts that exemplify this are *kaizen* and *ikigai*—terms that have recently gained buzz in Silicon Valley boardrooms and TED Talks alike. But in those environments, the meaning of the words are often stripped of their original context. While these Japanese words are now wielded as trendy productivity hacks or feel-good slogans, their roots tell a richer, more nuanced story about purpose, discipline, and harmony. In this chapter, I want to return these concepts to their source—not to gatekeep them, but to illuminate how they reflect a deeper philosophy of leadership. By exploring the real meaning of *ikigai* (one's reason for being) and *kaizen* (continuous, humble improvement), we can begin to understand what it means to lead from the inside—grounded in culture, attuned to others, and mindful of a nation's place in the world.

EMBRACING MY *IKIGAI*

Fully embracing my *ikigai* as a bridge-builder between the US and Japan, I joined Japan Society in December 2019 as the youngest president and CEO in the organization's history. I came almost immediately from my previous job at the Eurasia Group, where only a year before I had launched the first GZERO Summit in Tokyo. I arrived at Japan Society with a mandate for change—to make the organization more relevant in a global context, not just in New York. But no sooner had I moved my family to New York from Washington, DC, than the COVID closures began, and along with the rest of New York City's cultural organizations, Japan Society's focus turned toward survival.

In the summer of 2020, at the height of the COVID pandemic, I learned that I was a recipient of the 16th Nakasone Yasuhiro Award from the Nakasone Peace Institute in Tokyo. I was being honored not for my work or my position with Japan Society, but for my earlier research which uncovered under-appreciated points of connection between Japan and Türkiye, Europe, the Middle East, and Central Asia. The award was contingent on flying to Tokyo to meet with the leadership of the Nakasone Peace Institute, Japan's first major think-tank of its type that is focused on Japan's global role—something that is near and dear to my heart as a bridge-builder and a global citizen.

FAMILY CONNECTIONS

In the same way that Jimmy Carter was the first US president to become known for his post-presidency service, Yasuhiro Nakasone was a larger-than-life presence who, even after he had served as prime minister, maintained an outsized influence. Like Jimmy Carter, Nakasone lived to be nearly one hundred and had a significant impact on every single politician over several generations as well as the Liberal Democratic Party (LDP). During my childhood in Japan, my concept of US-Japan was shaped by the "Ron-Yasu" relationship, so termed because President Ronald Reagan was on a first-name basis with Yasuhiro Nakasone, Japan's longest serving prime minister at that time. I really wanted to accept the award in person. It wasn't practical, nor was it possible. Since I had family living in Japan it would have meant enduring a mandatory two-week quarantine. I was expecting to be turned down when I said that I was unable to come in person, but because all the other recipients, who were Japanese, were able to attend, I was able to have my parents accept the award on my behalf.

I sent a video message, with the first half in Japanese and the second half in English, something novel at that time which went over well with the audience, and my father ended up sitting next to Yasuhiro Nakasone's son, Hirofumi Nakasone, who had been foreign minister of Japan under Tarō Asō and who was the chair of the Nakasone Peace Institute. The president of the Institute at the time was my good friend, Ichiro Fujisaki, president of the America-Japan Society (Japan Society's sister organization in Tokyo) and a former ambassador for Japan to the United States. I believe that it was Ambassador Fujisaki who had tapped me for the award well before I joined Japan Society. When my father accepted the award on my behalf, he offered a few remarks in Japanese rather than just saying "thank you" and taking photographs as was customary. Making that family connection, with Nakasone's son presenting the award and my father receiving it, truly felt like a family honor. Receiving the Nakasone Yasuhiro Award gave me a lot of encouragement during this time, which was not an easy period for any of us. It was a validation of the path I had chosen for myself before I had joined Japan Society and a confirmation that I was following my *ikigai*.

JAPANESE AND AMERICAN *IKIGAI*

The term *ikigai* is not a simple word. It is often translated or mistranslated as "purpose"—and of course "purpose" can also have multiple meanings. When I think about *ikigai*, it's more about a motivating force, what animates a person's being or why that person exists in the world. That's the same concept I use when I think about the reasons why Japan and the United States, for example, exist. Japan is, and has always been, Japan—it is one of the most ancient civilizations that can trace its origins back to the beginning of human history. In contrast, America emerged as an independent nation 250 years ago as the colonists rebelled against the Europeans who had originally come over to settle land where Indigenous people had been living for thousands of years.

Our own national narratives, no matter our native country, color our reasons for being and our existence as societies. *Ikigai*, by definition, is a motivating force that creates something, so the question of "Why does Japan exist" is simply not asked. Japan's *ikigai*—its reason for being—is quietly profound: it exists because it exists. It exists not to dominate or expand, but to endure, refine, and find meaning in the continuity of its culture, its people, and its place in the world.

On the other hand, Americans often ask why the United States should continue to exist. America continually seeks to become a more perfect union by improving itself—which, appropriately, is the definition of *kaizen*. Japan as a country is deeply rooted in its past history and tradition while America's motiving force has always been freedom and the pursuit of happiness, a direct response to throwing off the yoke of the British Empire and emerging an independent nation in 1776.

For Americans, freedom is both a national and an individual narrative, with Americans questioning democracy almost every day. In Japan, *ikigai* is very much a personal journey about what makes a person happy and what their ultimate purpose is. It is not a national identity—it is more like a Venn diagram of what gives a person happiness and meaning in their life, not what they are good at doing or what profits them materially. This has become an attractive concept to Americans if you look at how many books now include this title and how often *ikigai* has been used in English—much like *omakase*, which, in New York, has taken on its own meaning, not of "chef's choice," but of "very expensive." My own concept of *ikigai*, however, is essentially Japanese. It is something that is almost innate to who I am, because I am uniquely situated as both an insider and an outsider in Japan and have spent so much of my life living on the edge of two worlds. I didn't find my *ikigai*; my *ikigai* found me.

SMOKE AND MIRRORS

Japanese are often surprised by how reactive and restive Americans can be. America's story is one of constant motion—a pendulum that swings not only in our politics, from left to right and back again, but also in our business dealings, where cycles of boom and bust, disruption and consolidation, define the rhythm of our economy. Japan certainly has historical rhythms but the cycles of history there tend to be judged in centuries rather than America's standard four- to twelve-year periods dictated by our presidential elections. Meanwhile, the concept of the American Dream has been sold to Japan ever since its defeat in World War II. The export of the American Dream to Japan enabled an economic miracle that was first showcased during the Tokyo Olympics in 1964 and then during the 1970 Osaka Expo. Although the miracle challenged the American system in the 1980s, collapsing after the burst of Japan's economic bubble, it reemerged fully charged again thirty years later. It is unrealistic to impose the romanticized American Dream of two cars and a white picket fence on Japan because, not in the least, it literally wouldn't fit onto the island! Even in the US today, the American Dream is not quite realistic. Many Americans feel that they are not better off than their parents or their grandparents. Yet many people around the world still associate the American Dream with continual progress.

Using the US-Japan relationship as a mirror, what do we see when we hold the mirror up to ourselves? One of the most interesting things about a mirror is that we think that everything is an accurate reflection. Actually, a mirror reflects us backwards, and our eyes adjust for the difference. For Japan and the US the first images we see are opposites—an island nation versus a continental power, a society that thinks of itself as a collective versus a society that thinks of itself as a country of individuals. But when we go beyond the *genkan*, or lobby, of both countries, there are a lot more similarities than meet the eye. We need to know how to look at each other in that mirror and learn from it. America may be very individualistic but we also project a subtly collective outlook. As as a result, Americans thrive when united by a common purpose rather than when they are fractured by an internal divide. As rugged individualists, Americans are great at big picture strategy, but we don't do as well in the execution phase because there are too many independent players in the operational mix. Japanese leaders have historically been more comfortable executing big-picture strategy than crafting it—preferring to operate within established frameworks rather than assertively designing them. Nowhere is this more evident than in the US-Japan security architecture. After World War II, Japan adopted a pacifist constitution and entrusted the broader strategic direction of its defense policy to the United States under the security alliance. While Japan has excelled at adapting, implementing, and optimizing within that alliance—building one of the world's most sophisticated self-defense forces and hosting key US military bases—it has largely refrained from initiating bold strategic shifts on its own. This reflects a broader cultural tendency toward consensus, caution, and incrementalism—values that prioritize harmony over disruption and execution over ideological authorship. As a result Japan is able to look at America holistically in a way that we cannot see ourselves. Our divisions, which seem to us to be polar opposites, reflect in Japan's mirror as the yin and the yang, or the head and the tail, of one America.

CHAPTER TEN

KAIZEN AND UNDERSTANDING HARMONY IN JAPAN

The stereotype of Japan as a nation that prizes conformity over individualism stems from centuries of cultural evolution shaped by geography, demography, and social necessity. As an island nation with limited natural resources and densely populated, habitable land, Japan developed a societal ethic that prioritized group cohesion over individual expression. In such close quarters, *wa*, or harmony, wasn't just a cultural preference—it became a survival strategy. This emphasis on social balance gave rise to customs of indirect communication, hierarchical respect, and a deep aversion to standing out in ways that might disrupt the group. But what may appear as conformity to outsiders is understood in Japan as something deeper: a harmony of being that aligns with the concept of *ikigai*, or one's reason for living. In the Japanese context, *ikigai* is not simply about personal fulfillment—it is about finding joy and meaning in a way that supports, rather than disturbs, the well-being of others. It reflects a collective sense of purpose, where true happiness is measured not just by individual achievement, but by how gently one's own life fits into the lives of others.

By naming the 232nd era of its official calendar *Reiwa*, meaning "beautiful harmony," Japan has chosen harmony as its official mission statement. As citizens of a relatively young nation historically grounded in wide-open spaces and opportunities, Americans feel quite the opposite—that an individual has a right to do what they want—the right to life, liberty, and pursuit of happiness, as the Declaration of Independence so memorably puts it—at the same time looking outwards for opportunity rather than inside, as the Japanese do. Americans are constantly trying to change their reality, whereas in Japan people live in the moment, accepting their own purpose and being since things can change at any time, as indeed they have over history. The difference is palpable in American and Japanese business culture and etiquette: Americans wish to get to the point of a meeting as quickly and efficiently as possible, whereas Japanese doing business spend the majority of their time not directly discussing the matter at hand. Understanding the societal roots of our cultural differences, both business and personal, can go a long way toward improving our relationships.

KAIZEN AT WORK

There is no definitive English translation for *kaizen*. "Continuous self-improvement" might be the best interpretation. In Japanese *kaizen* is essentially one word with a powerful set of underlying assumptions and meanings. In the ecosystems of American startup culture and business, the term *kaizen* has now become ubiquitous. This started in the 1980s when Toyota was identified as using what was called the *kaizen* system, which allowed individual workers to improve on industrial processes without needing top-down authorization. If a worker saw a detail that wasn't right, they could bring the entire assembly line to a halt to correct it. This practice was something not only respected by management but also encouraged and incentivized. Integral to the *kaizen* system is the concept that every person is responsible for everything around them. You cannot only blame a leader for a problem—and you yourself must be part of the solution. This is very much in line with Japan's history of having a system in place for centuries that fosters a need for continuous self-improvement.

In Japanese culture, small incremental changes effected over large cycles of time are more realistic than big changes in short periods of time. In the US, we tend to be fixated on that big moment—the moment of transformation from idea to product, setting goals that lead directly to change and transformation. We want to master our environment. This practice assumes that resources are unlimited and the trajectory of change is linear. In contrast, Japan values careful stewardship of its limited natural resources. The Japanese also embrace the fact that change is cyclical—that every end precedes a new beginning.

SYSTEMS AND RESOURCES

Americans tend to be less concerned with how one person's actions impact other people. We have a saying: "That's not my problem." In Japan, the shared concept of *kaizen* points to the fact that people are all interconnected in some way. These connections, interwoven throughout society and business, mean that a person must at least consider the actions of others and the impact of their own actions, whether immediate or in the time to come. *Kaizen* did not start as a business term; it was meant to explain the world around us and how we find our place there. Reduced to a Western business context, *kaizen* is used as a tool to measure the output of a business and those working there. This is something that I struggle with as a political scientist, because while I understand the need to measure output and for human beings to have a metric for success, sometimes the greatest successes in life cannot actually be identified until later on. For example, what makes us richer in the end is not necessarily about how much money you've made in your life; it might be how you raise your children, or your relationships, or certain quiet moments, and taking time to help someone in need.

GEOPOLITICS AND TECHNOLOGY

Technological shifts are rapidly changing the world, including the way that people relate within and outside of our societies. But *kaizen* doesn't really address the tools of society. Whether we're talking about the invention of the wheel or a semiconductor chip, *kaizen* in Japan is a philosophy and a way of being. Japan has the advantage over the US as an early adopter of technology and technological fads, something that happens much more quickly and easily because of its homogenous population, and it lacks some of the ethical issues around robots and machines that seem to be prevalent in American society. Yet that same ease of use and the Japanese concepts of happiness and success can also lead to stagnation instead of innovation. Americans, on the other hand, just keep on innovating, because in our consumer culture no one is ever fully satisfied. Nor are Americans mindful of the needs of others, something that has only increased the extreme divide between the "haves" and the "have nots" in our country. There is an opportunity here to bring the true concept of *kaizen*, not just its one-sided productivity models, into the American system.

There's also an opportunity here for Japan, which has something far greater to offer the world on the international stage than just aligning with American strategic leadership. It is deeply rooted in Japanese culture that people can and should be part of the process of stepping around their leaders for the sake of incremental improvement. Japanese society isn't set up to produce clones of Prime Minister Abe or Prime Minister Nakasone, so this means working beyond existing leadership to participate in the international community within both the business and geopolitical arenas in a call to action to safeguard our rapidly changing world.

IKIGAI IN GOVERNMENT SERVICE

Both the US State Department and the Japanese Foreign Ministry are staffed by highly qualified people dedicated to each of their countries' respective missions. To take a job in the Ministry of Foreign Affairs is not necessarily to follow your *ikigai*—it's a forty-year career path where, if everything is done right and you keep your head down, perhaps one day you'll become an ambassador. That's the *ikigai* of the position—it's the ultimate outcome, not the mission itself. American Foreign Service workers do not hesitate to leave, whether during a period of self-evaluation at the ten-year mark, as also happens in the US military, or as a resignation in protest against government action, as with the war in Iraq under George W. Bush's presidency. Yet no matter what happened in Japan, including major disruptions and challenges that Japan faced in the early 2000s—whether it was 9/11 and the Afghanistan mission, or the war in Iraq, or when Japan for the first time sent foreign service officers and Self-Defense Forces to support American operations around the world—few in the Japanese bureaucracy resigned or even protested.

Americans in the public sector look at their calling and purpose in a much larger way. Their *ikigai* is the larger mission of America's role in the world, which I don't think the Japanese Foreign Ministry treats the same way. Perhaps that is a function of a parliamentary system versus a presidential system, but I think it has a lot to do with how American and Japanese diplomats see their missions. The American diplomats that I've worked with over the years are on the whole extremely self-confident and vocal, and even though the US military may have seen more actions (and certainly more funding), it is the diplomats who are constantly being called on to try to find ways of mitigating and increasing America's role in the world. In the Japanese context, diplomats are bureaucrats who almost never are able to take that step forward to have agency. You must have agency to be able to believe that you are a part of that larger calling which is *ikigai*.

PART THREE

REIMAGINING LEADERSHIP

Prescriptions for Japan's Global Role and the Alliance's Future

CHAPTER ELEVEN

LEADERSHIP AND HISTORY

Prime Minister Shinzo Abe (1954-2022) is now remembered as a truly exceptional leader. Taking office for the second time in 2012 together with the LDP's sweeping return to power after the 3.11 disasters, and informed by his own first short-lived tenure as prime minister in 2006-2007, he and his team were actually able to learn from and then make bureaucracy work better for Japan. His simple proposition was that he had to be able to explain what Japan needed to be doing better on the global stage, and that meant having self-confidence. In his own unique and very Japanese way, Prime Minister Abe started where every leader needs to start: by inspiring the Japanese people to believe in Japan.

As Japan's longest serving prime minister, and the only prime minister to return to office since Prime Minister Shigeru Yoshida in 1948, Shinzo Abe's leadership and his service to Japan were deeply consequential. He was also a friend of mine and of Japan Society. He visited the Society many times over the years, and his interactions always showed his curiosity and his incredible people skills. In 2015, Prime Minister Abe addressed a joint session of Congress as the first Japanese prime minister ever to do so. In a speech titled, "Toward an Alliance of Hope," Abe articulated his own personal history as the son of a foreign minister and the grandson of a war criminal who came back to become prime minister of Japan and shape the course of US-Japan relations. For me, Prime Minister Abe personalized leadership and the US-Japan relationship with a grace and power that may never be matched.

AMERICAN-STYLE LEADERSHIP

There's a feeling sometimes in the world that Americans are arrogant and that we act like cowboys. I hadn't really seen this arrogance up close and personal until my work in Türkiye, when American diplomats and military officers would go into a meeting with a Turkish delegation filled with smiles, only to denigrate the Turks behind the scenes afterwards. To me, that felt very disingenuous. I understood the need for diplomats to keep their cards close to their chest. But I also really respected and deeply appreciated the people and culture that we were dealing with. Given Türkiye's long imperial history, complex regional entanglements, and deep-seated memories of Western intervention during the Ottoman Empire and formation of the modern republic, Turks may at times withhold full information or view America's ambitions in the Middle East with suspicion. Their behavior is shaped by a legacy of geopolitical maneuvering in which they've often felt more like subjects than partners of global strategy.

One of the challenges that American leaders face is that they are in some ways the king of the hill but with a target on their backs. America certainly hasn't shown our best examples of diplomacy in the Middle East. But ultimately, when people retire, whether politicians, business leaders, or diplomats, they no longer have that veneer in front of them which prevents them from telling the truth. I often wonder whether it's the moment that shapes the leader or whether it's the leader who shapes the moment. Former President Bill Clinton made famous the concept that if he had been born at the same time as FDR, maybe he would have been as consequential, but instead of World War II he had to deal with Yugoslavia. Clinton wanted to be that consequential president, but he never quite got the same kind of foreign policy opportunity that George W. Bush had after 9/11. It also matters who you are and how you respond. I saw some of the best of America when I heard President Barack Obama address the Turkish parliament—the first African American president telling the entire world that America is not a perfect union, it's a more perfect union.

THEORIES OF LEADERSHIP

For a Japanese businessperson to understand what drives America, they must know that American sensibilities are fundamentally different from Japanese in terms of defining both national and personal purpose. The difference lies in contrasting concepts of "being." Americans often define "being" in relation to something else—through achievement, opposition, or reaction to the world around them—whereas in Japan, "being" is understood more introspectively, rooted in one's relationship to self and inner purpose rather than defined by contrast with the "other." American history, and much of Western history in general, works on the theory that one "great man," one single leader, changed the course of history. Without George Washington or King George III, whose actions paved the way for American independence in 1776, the United States might not exist in the way it does today.

In the 1560s, during one of the most fractured and violent periods in Japanese history, a young warlord named Oda Nobunaga began a campaign that would ultimately set Japan on a path toward unification. While history often remembers him as a ruthless military tactician and iconoclast, what truly set Nobunaga apart was not his strategy or ambition; it was the clarity of his personal *ikigai*. He believed that Japan could no longer survive under the rule of countless competing warlords, and he was driven relentlessly by his sense of purpose—rooted not in personal glory alone, but in restoring order to a nation in chaos. This inner drive, this reason for being, was not declared loudly, nor did it require the validation of the world. It was a force that emanated from within, shaping his leadership and legacy.

In doing so, Nobunaga exemplified a distinct model of leadership that contrasts sharply with the Western "great man" theory. In the Western tradition, leaders are often cast as individuals who shape history through charisma, conquest, or singular genius. But in Japanese culture, and indeed in the culture of many other Asian countries, leadership is often viewed more as the expression of a great philosophy—an alignment of individual will with the needs of society and the harmony of civilization. Nobunaga's leadership was not just about defeating rivals; it was about dismantling old systems to pave the way for a unified, stable Japan—something larger than himself. He sparked a process completed by Toyotomi Hideyoshi and Tokugawa Ieyasu—the two other "Great Unifiers" of Japan—but it began with one man's deep, uncompromising sense of *ikigai*.

As we reflect on the meaning of leadership in today's world—amid uncertainty, fragmentation, and rising polarization—Nobunaga's example reminds us that the most lasting change often starts not with dominance, but with purpose. True leadership does not require a loud voice or a sweeping ideology. Sometimes, it begins quietly, with a leader deeply in touch with his or her inner compass. *Ikigai* teaches us that leadership, at its best, emerges not from the desire to be great, but from the commitment to be useful—to oneself, to one's people, and to the course of history.

INSIDER OR OUTSIDER?

So, we return to where we began: that by necessity, all leaders must be insiders. If you don't understand the country or the organization that you lead, you're not going to be able to keep that position. On the other hand, there is value in an outsider perspective that allows a person to connect beyond their leadership role, so that the "yes man" philosophy or the "great leader" philosophy does not become paramount. The terms insider and outsider beg the question about belonging and what that means to each person within a particular society. Throughout our lives, we're asked to define ourselves and put ourselves in certain boxes. Yet as human beings, we all want to find ways of belonging. History has many lessons to teach us about that, looking from both the insider and the outsider perspectives, and also by examining closed and open societies. Without all of these pieces, there cannot be evolution or progress.

CHAPTER TWELVE

UNDERSTANDING DEMOCRACY

For a political scientist, democracy is a complex and nebulous concept. It's more than just about voting. It is also about the political governance of people. In this chapter we will explore democracy in the US and Japan through the lens of each society's political structures and societal organization.

RULES AND PRECEDENTS

Japanese society is guided by an unwritten set of rules rooted in harmony, hierarchy, and social obligation—principles that shape behavior across business, political leadership, and everyday cultural interactions. In the US, there are a lot of laws and rules but the limits of these documents, from the Articles of Confederation to the Constitution, haven't actually been challenged in the way that is happening under the current Trump administration. Along with term limits for presidents, America has certain things that have always been done and understood in a certain way. What has come to be thought of as the modern presidency is founded on the precedents of George Washington and the Founding Fathers, for example. Today, those founding precedents are being undone because the president can choose to act a certain way and, as the current argument seems to go, whatever the president does is, by definition, legal. This is a very litigious challenge to the American democratic system and a country built on law.

In Japan, on the other hand, social norms can be as powerful as the written law. It's not about what's written in the Japanese constitution, it's about what is expected of every Japanese and what makes them Japanese. In Japan, social norms emphasize duty, respect for hierarchy, group harmony, and self-restraint—values instilled from an early age that define what is expected of every Japanese person and form the core of a shared national identity. In the US, because we come from so many different places and there is so much diversity of thought, there is a process—both legal and societal—of constant challenge and constant compromise.

We often talk about democracy in terms of equal say for everyone, but the United States is becoming a place where some people have more say than others. One of the big differences between the US and Japan is that American democracy, by definition, is messier and doesn't conform to a fixed structural process in the same way as Japan. In Japan, the head of the Keidanren or Keizai Dōyukai and the Japanese Business Federation are voices that speaks on behalf of much of the business community. In the US we also have the Chamber of Commerce and the Business Roundtable, and other such groups. But, as we're seeing right now, the president increasingly can choose whom he wants to represent business. If the president wants the representatives of business to be a bunch of tech billionaires, he can effect that, even for a short period of time, as with Elon Musk. In Japan, that matters a lot and the selection of people to represent business interests is ironically both more democratic and more process-driven. While Japan may feel more top-down due to its strong emphasis on hierarchical relationships, centralized decision-making within organizations and cultural values prioritize respect for authority and consensus from senior leadership. Leaders are typically selected through internal consensus within political parties and seniority-based systems, emphasizing group harmony and gradual advancement, in contrast to America's more direct presidential mandate and voter-driven electoral process.

PARTY SYSTEM

Japan's conservative coalition has dominated the country's party system for most of the postwar period. In fact, the running joke about the Liberal Democratic Party is that it is neither liberal or democratic. It started during the Cold War period as an amalgamation of right-leaning business interests originally brought together to try to keep Japan on course for the sake of the US-Japan alliance. That original one-party system is now manifesting in a very different way.

The election of Prime Minister Ishiba was the first of its kind in a post-faction world where the LDP had a very unusual election for their leader that was basically decided in a populist method inside of the LDP that was quickly followed by that of Prime Minister Takaichi. That's not using "populist" in the same sense as the American Electoral College, of course, but it is still a unique occurrence. Japan is one of the only places where weakness is a strength. Japan's constitution has endured since the end of the American Occupation and there is a reason that it hasn't been replaced. That is spelled out explicitly in the Yoshida Doctrine right after the war, when Japan as a country without military power was able to use that to its advantage in garnering American economic support. The geopolitical landscape has, of course, changed dramatically in the last seventy-plus years, but even after, Ishiba's perceived weakness made it possible to face few serious challengers compared to what he would face in other countries. In most democracies and parliamentary systems, when somebody is weak, like Canada's Justin Trudeau, he is removed from office by mass opposition. But in Japan, precisely because of a leader's weakness or unpopularity, like Ishiba's, he is able to hang on far longer than expected even after suffering electoral defeats. The real question is when an exception emerges who can actually lead which leads to the present-day prime minister that is already making history as Japan's first female leader who also happened to be Prime Minister Abe's protégé. She is in good company given that exceptions to the rule in Japan have been former prime ministers: Abe, Koizumi, Nakasone, and Yoshida—all of whom have left their mark through their relationships with US presidents. The relationship between prime minister and US president is the most important metric of Japanese success in postwar foreign policy therefore the attention on Takaichi and Trump's chemistry will continue to be of critical bilateral and global interest.

PERSONALITY SYSTEM

Unlike the US, Japan does not have a term limit for its prime minister, but historically, it's almost impossible to keep the support of the party leader beyond a couple of years. Although the conservative-leaning Liberal Democratic Party of Japan (LDP) has demonstrated its ability to hold power over several decades, there's always been a reset every few years. We saw this just before 3.11, when the opposition party came in expressing its dissatisfaction with the LDP but without thinking that there would be any real change of leadership. What's interesting today is that the main leader of the CDP, the opposition party, is Yoshihiko Noda, who was prime minister from 2011 to 2012. This is a uniquely weak moment for Japan today at a time when its leadership should be more relevant and manifested. Although Japan's soft power is burgeoning, it does not have the political leadership needed to flourish in the world today.

Japan today stands at a pivotal moment—uniquely positioned to lead not through force, but through example. What Japan needs now is leadership that embraces its enduring political stability as a platform for global engagement, not insularity. In a world increasingly divided and searching for direction, Japan's strength lies in its ability to lead with humility, consistency, and cultural depth. The country's natural soft power—from its globally resonant content and traditions to its reputation for quality, civility, and consensus—offers a powerful counterbalance to the chaos and polarization seen in America. Japan should lean into this distinct identity, championing a model of leadership that prizes human connection, long-term thinking, and cultural authenticity. The world doesn't need more muscle—it needs meaning. And few nations are better suited than Japan to provide this.

FUNDAMENTAL DIFFERENCES

There are other fundamental differences between democracy in the United States and democracy in Japan. In the US, the "rule of law" basically refers to how power is projected and how it is used by leaders. The three co-equal branches of government—the Executive, the Legislative, and the Judicial—comprise a unique system in which the president might be "first among equals," not least for his ability because of being able to nominate any incoming justices to serve on the Supreme Court. However, those justices are voted on by the legislature, and although the president may be the commander-in-chief, the funds to execute on pretty much any other priority are held by the legislature. That system of checks and balances is usually what is meant by "the rule of law" on a federal scale. Ultimately, the highest form of that rule of law is the Constitution of the United States, and to amend the Constitution is an incredibly high hurdle. No president has the authority to rewrite the Constitution, although they might hold great power in other areas. The debate that is currently happening in the US about the rule of law is whether those co-equal branches can exist in a world in which one personality dominates one party and the opposing party is not functioning as a natural force in the American system of checks and balances.

Voting in Japan and the United States reflects fundamentally different political structures and civic cultures. In the US, elections are held at multiple levels—federal, state, and local—with considerable variation in voting rules and access depending on the state. Citizens vote directly for a wide range of officials, from the president and members of Congress to governors, judges, school board members, and even sheriffs, making civic participation more frequent but also more complex. In contrast, Japan operates under a more centralized system: National elections determine members of the Diet, while prefectural and municipal elections are more streamlined and less frequent. Voting in Japan is non-compulsory, held on Sundays, and largely paper-based, with a strong emphasis on order and procedure. While Japanese citizens vote directly for local and national legislators, they do not vote for the prime minister, who is selected by the Diet. As a result, the average Japanese citizen tends to experience politics more passively, with less participatory agency than in the (albeit sometimes chaotic) American system.

In Japan, the parliamentary system was strengthened by a constitution drafted under the heavy influence of the American Occupation, alongside the creation of the Liberal Democratic Party, the ruling party in Japan since 1955 to the present day. The factions in the LDP determined the democratic norms, and cooperation between the business and political elites—which Americans might view as collusion—led to a cohesive and harmonious society in Japan. While elections in Japan have always determined who gets to serve in the Diet's House of Representatives and the House of Councillors. who gets to become prime minister is usually determined by a smaller group of party leaders. The American system is very much based on "one vote, one person." Voting, the American thinking goes, is what makes one a citizen. Voting is like a national holiday in some ways and it is also very much impacted by both traditional and social media. In Japan, voting is a kind of mechanism that acknowledges the country's power centers and the status quo. On the other hand, democracy in the US is in a constant process of evolution and compromise, something that has always been the American way but has more recently become a dirty word. In Japan, democracy is simply the way that things get done and a natural extension of societal consensus and harmony where the individual leader is less important than the party. It's traditionally been a party system where things get done in back rooms, and that is the norm that is now being challenged. In the US, until recently, there's been a strong focus on exposing the back rooms and trying to get as many people of all kinds involved as possible, sometimes at the expense of the educated elites who are also part of the American democratic system.

THE ROLE OF NONPROFITS

The role of nonprofit organizations in the US is in many ways uniquely American. One of the things that I look to for inspiration as Japan Society's leader is how my predecessor, John D. Rockefeller III, spoke about the nonprofit sector as the "third way"—the idea that nonprofits play a critical role in between the government and the business community. Whether the focus is on arts and culture or civic engagement and education, there needs to be another group looking out for the best interests of our citizens, not just for the sake of profit or national interest.

This is why nonprofits and the role of civil society are very much engrained in the American approach to democracy. As a nonprofit organization Japan Society exists in some ways as a public good that the private sector pays for through its donations and contributions. Yet the Society cannot be bought, per se, and although we certainly welcome partnerships and collaboration, these must always align with our mission. The fact that Japan Society is based in New York and not Washington, DC, also lets us play a larger role, because New York City in some ways operates as a global stage for the international community.

STUDYING DEMOCRACY

In 2016, during a six-month period as a Presidential Leadership Scholar, I studied democracy in action, learning about national leadership from past presidents as well as the then-current administration. The creation of the Presidential Leadership Scholars program is a uniquely American story that traces its roots to the unlikely friendship between Bill Clinton and George H.W. Bush. Clinton, a young Southern governor, defeated the establishment Republican candidate George H.W. Bush and went on to have a tumultuous tenure that included scandals and trouble with both Democrats and Republicans, most famously Newt Gingrich. Yet, after that experience, when George H.W. Bush's son, George W. Bush, took office as president at the end of Clinton's second four-year term, both Bill Clinton and George H.W. Bush were asked by George W. Bush to serve in various capacities, including in the 2004 Indonesian tsunami relief effort and the period immediately after Hurrican Katrina. An unlikely friendship began between these two former presidents, despite their having competed against each other for the leadership of the country.

The guiding concept of the Presidential Leadership Scholars program, which launched in 2015, was that four presidential libraries— those of

Lyndon B. Johnson, George H.W. Bush, William J. Clinton, and George W. Bush—should take an active part in educating future American leaders. I was part of the second class of Presidential Leadership Scholars, in 2016, a tumultuous year in US politics when Hillary Clinton was running for president while major protests erupted in Ferguson, Missouri. We were sixty Americans drawn from all parts of the US, nominated not only by the presidential libraries but also from regional hubs to ensure equal representation from all states and regions. Most people taking part were from all walks of life, and I believe that I was one of the few individuals selected on the basis of being international even I hailed from the Virginia/DC area. I was nominated by Bill Richardson, who had been US ambassador to the United Nations and secretary of energy under the Clinton administration. I had been working with him as part of APCO's International Advisory Council and he'd seen the program and recommended that I apply for the program as a natural fit.

Over the course of six months, we met with former presidents Bill Clinton and George H.W. Bush as well as President George W. Bush and their respective cabinets. Listening to the presidents themselves articulate their visions of leadership, it all boiled down to the fact that even though they may have had ideological differences, what made them so unique was the American experience of compromise and working together. Our required reading, *The Presidents Club: Inside the World's Most Exclusive Fraternity*, by Nancy Gibbs and Michael Duffy, talks about how, once you've been president, the way you see the world is very much shaped from a perspective of deeper understanding. Instead of criticizing their successors, the Presidents Club usually stayed together and would reconnect at world events and other significant occasions.

For our graduation, the first-year class was also invited back, and we went to Little Rock, Arkansas. Our graduation ceremony took place at Little Rock Central High School, where the Little Rock Nine had desegregated Little Rock Central High School in September 1957.

Former British Prime Minister Tony Blair was the guest of honor, speaking alongside Bill Clinton and George W. Bush. Then, along came a tornado. As I wrote in the *Huffington Post* in 2016:

> It sounded like a train rolling through a station or a powerful earthquake shaking the historic Central High School of Little Rock as three world leaders looked up with three members of the famous Little Rock Nine and everyone else in the auditorium. Mark Updegrove, President of the LBJ Library, who was delivering the final speech of the day, quickly closed with, 'Good Luck and Godspeed' before giving instructions for everyone to seek shelter from the tornado that had touched down on our graduation ceremony. In many ways, it was a fitting and timely ending for the Presidential Leadership Scholars of 2016's tenure.

The people in my class have become lifelong friends who are doing amazing things. It really was a humbling experience because when you do international affairs like I do, and when you focus on countries like Japan that I care so deeply about, you realize that for the average American, the whole world is not their world. Most people are necessarily concerned with their own local world. For me, the US-Japan relationship is local, but to the average American, their community is everything. Japan is physically very far away from America, so the only way to make Japan and the US-Japan relationship real is to find that human connection, that *kizuna*.

INTERCONNECTIVITY AND IMPACT

Since my time as a Presidential Leadership Scholar, significant changes in global communications have given rise to a more interconnected world in which news, in particular, travels very quickly. I would argue that the media had a significant impact on recent elections in both the US and Japan, especially in 2024 with the reelection of President Trump and the election of Prime Minister Ishiba, after which he lost control of his party and government. That Ishiba was able to remain as prime minister at all is a function of not just the mood of the Japanese people, but the way that the media and LDP felt about him during the election—that he was the "least worst" choice. With Trump's first term in 2016, his win was unexpected—he was more of a media darling and a fascination, someone who brought up the ratings of news networks just like his own reality TV show. By 2024, the media had become one of Trump's favorite tools and targets, and he chose which outlets would cover him favorably and which would not, consistently and incessantly attacking the unfavorable ones, whether *The New York Times*, MSNBC, or CNN. This then became part of the larger narrative that brought the MAGA movement to power in 2024.

Social media also played a huge role in the 2024 American presidential election. Social media still plays a far less influential role in Japanese elections compared to the United States, largely due to cultural norms, legal restrictions, and the enduring power of traditional media. Until 2013, Japan had strict laws limiting online electioneering, which slowed the adoption of digital platforms for political campaigning. Even today, Japanese political discourse on social media remains relatively restrained, reflecting broader societal values of harmony, discretion, and deference to established authority. In contrast, American elections are deeply shaped by social media, where candidates and voters alike use platforms aggressively to mobilize support, frame narratives, and challenge opponents. In Japan, however, traditional media—particularly television, newspapers, and NHK, the state-run TV network—continues to be the dominant source of political information, trusted for its neutrality and formality. As a result, while social media may shape younger voters' perceptions and definitely had an impact with the rise of the far right nationalist Sanseitō in the Upper House elections of 2025, it has not yet disrupted the entire structure or tone of Japanese electoral politics in the way it has transformed the United States.

CHAPTER THIRTEEN

DEMOCRACY TODAY

Today, politics, and by extension, geopolitics, can no longer be separated from the media. Consider how an educated, informed citizenry makes its choice about who should be leader. In most of our democracies, it's not about making the best choice; it's about making the least worst choice.

THE 2024 US PRESIDENTIAL ELECTION

That President Trump beat Kamala Harris is no surprise, nor was Harris' last-minute substitution for President Biden on the Democratic presidential ticket. Trump took advantage of the populist mood during his campaign with many key moments, including an attempted assassination, but given the shortened contest against Harris he seemed to have the structural advantage. Ishiba was elected leader of the LDP seemingly out of the blue to prevent Sanae Takaichi's brand of conservativism, because Kishida had not been expected to step down. Everyone in the US-Japan space was surprised when that happened but it seemed almost to be in response to President Biden's own withdrawal from the presidential race. While history will ultimately reveal how closely interconnected these two separate political calculations were, the underlying discontent and trends against incumbency or insiders at the expense of more "populist" outsiders is clear. The only question is whether Kishida re-emerges as a force just like Abe once did.

When Ishiba was selected as LDP leader, that election was based not just on his popularity; it was also a reaction against Takaichi's brand of rightwing conservatism. Now after a series of lost elections and the rise of rightwing populist opposition parts the LDP is embracing Takaichi. In many ways, Ishiba's election mirrored the election of Trump, which in 2016 was a dual reaction to both America's first African American president and America's first female major candidate. In 2024, the election of Trump seemed to be a reaction, at least in part, to the fact that his opposition was the first African American female candidate in American history. Takaichi's story is only now being written.

2024 ELECTIONS IN JAPAN

In the Japanese parliamentary system, there are no set terms like in the US presidential system, which grants a minimum of four years for one term. In Ishiba's case, less than a month after his LDP presidential victory he went to the polls to get a verdict from the people. There, he lost further seats. Then less than a year later, in the Upper House elections, he lost again. Although he wasn't removed from office, for the first time in many years the LDP has became a minority government, setting up another Abe-like scenario of needing to find a leader to lead the LDP back to power in the face of a divided and weak opposition.

Often the most observed relationship in US-Japan is how our two leaders interact personally despite the differences in our systems. Prime Minister Ishiba's initial visit to President Trump at the White House on February 7, 2025, was a huge success as Trump praised Ishiba in a way that the world—and Ishiba himself—had never seen before. Of course, this reflects more of an individual calculation by the president as this seems to be part of Trump's modus operandi in general—to always make sure that his opponent is built up so that he can have the upper hand. But President Trump in some ways guaranteed that Ishiba would last as prime minister beyond what domestic politics would have allowed, which was not the case before that visit. This again speaks to the interconnectivity and the linkages between both our democracies and our elections.

Because Japan is the largest investor in the United States, it has a major impact on how the America economy will flourish, or not. Likewise, we need to consider Japan's responses vis-à-vis US policy, whether relating to tariffs, the dismantling of the trade world to which we are accustomed, rethinking the world order beyond a post-World War II environment, or reimagining what the US-Japan community can be in a time of radical change. For all of us as individual citizens alongside non-governmental organizations such as Japan Society this is an opportunity to take on new roles in support of the US-Japan alliance.

JAPAN'S BUSINESS FOCUS

In the American vision of Japan, especially from the 1980s, few images are more iconic—or more misunderstood—than that of the Japanese businessman or *salaryman*: suited, stoic, riding a crowded train home well after dark, briefcase in hand, tie slightly loosened. This figure has become a symbol of Japan's postwar economic miracle and its corporate-driven society, embodying traits like discipline, loyalty, and sacrifice. But beneath the surface of this stereotype lies a deeper story about how Japan's economic culture is intertwined with its political structure, creating a system where business and governance are not only connected—they are often indistinguishable.

The roots of this obsession with business lie in Japan's rapid industrialization and its reconstruction after World War II. With national pride and economic survival at stake, work became more than just a means of livelihood; it was a civic duty. Corporations like Toyota, Mitsubishi, and Sony became national champions, and the *salaryman* became the human engine of Japan's rise. Lifetime employment and group loyalty were hallmarks of the system, and working long hours wasn't just expected—it was a reflection of identity and belonging.

THE WORK ETHIC AND THE POLITICAL ECONOMY

This cultural work ethic has always mirrored—and been reinforced by—Japan's political economy. The long-dominant LDP, in power almost consecutively since 1955, has historically aligned closely with big business and industry groups. Political influence is often secured through deep relationships with powerful economic actors, from construction firms to agricultural cooperatives. In return, these groups provide campaign donations, organizational muscle, and voting blocs. It's a system that functions less through overt corruption and more through implicit exchange: political access for economic support. Critics have called it "pay-to-play," not in the American sense of individual lobbying or dark money, but through an institutionalized form of political patronage built on long-term reciprocity.

This tight linkage between business and politics has profound consequences. It can foster stability, as seen in Japan's smooth bureaucratic policymaking and long-term infrastructure planning. But it also leads to complacency, cronyism, and limited innovation. Regulatory capture—where ministries act in the interest of the industries they oversee—is not uncommon, and newer or disruptive voices, including entrepreneurs, women, and younger voters, often find themselves shut out of the system.

While Japan has made attempts at political and economic reform, the cultural valorization of work and the political embeddedness of business remain deeply entrenched. In a rapidly changing global economy, the question is whether this model—built for a manufacturing-heavy, top-down, postwar society—can adapt to the demands of a more digital, decentralized, and inclusive future. In the end, the Japanese *salaryman* is not merely a stereotype, but a mirror of a society where work is still a stand-in for worth, and where power often flows not through ideas or elections alone—but through networks built at the intersection of boardrooms and the ballot box.

AMERICA'S SECURITY STATE AND THE POLITICS OF PROFIT

If Japan's postwar trajectory was defined by its obsession with business and corporate harmony, America's path has been shaped by a very different gravitational force: national security. Since World War II, and especially following the Cold War, the United States has prioritized military strength and global influence above all else, giving rise to a massive and enduring defense-industrial complex. While Japan's political system revolves around economic players and industry groups, America's politics have long been shaped by security contractors, intelligence agencies, and the sprawling network of public-private interests that sustain the machinery of global power.

The roots of this focus lie in geography and ideology. Protected by oceans and blessed with vast natural resources, the United States has never had to worry about invasion in the way Japan historically did. Instead, America exported its anxieties—fighting wars far from home, from Korea and Vietnam to Iraq and Afghanistan. Each conflict justified a growing web of defense spending, intelligence gathering, and military R&D. President Dwight D. Eisenhower warned in 1961 of the growing "military-industrial complex," a term that has since come to define the entangled relationship between the Pentagon, defense contractors like Lockheed Martin and Raytheon, and Congress itself. Entire districts and jobs depend on military spending, making it politically untouchable.

THE BUSINESS OF SECURITY

This emphasis on security has shaped America's business environment in fundamental ways. In contrast to Japan's consensus-driven *keiretsu* system and close public-private coordination, the US has encouraged competition, disruption, and private initiative—often funded through government contracts. Silicon Valley itself grew out of Cold War defense spending, with the Defense Advanced Research Projects Agency (DARPA) backing early innovations that led to the internet and modern computing. Even today, the biggest US tech firms—Google, Amazon, Microsoft—are deeply embedded in national security, from cloud infrastructure to AI development for defense applications.

However, the American system's rewards and risks are more extreme. While it fosters innovation and rapid growth, it also produces greater inequality and volatility. Entrepreneurs and venture capitalists thrive in an environment of risk-taking and government-backed research, but there's less stability and predictability than in Japan's corporate culture. Moreover, political access is often secured through campaign finance, lobbying, and PACs—creating a legal but often opaque "pay-to-play" structure that contrasts with Japan's more relationship-driven model.

Today, the landscape is shifting. As geopolitical threats evolve—from cybersecurity to climate-related instability—the lines between commercial tech and national defense are blurring. American companies once wary of working with the military are now re-engaging, while the government seeks to secure technological dominance in a new era of strategic competition, especially with China. In this environment, the American focus on security is starting to resemble Japan's traditional business-government alignment—only with more speed, scale, and global stakes.

Ultimately, while Japan's system has prized economic harmony and consensus, America's has prioritized strategic dominance and innovation through power. Doing business in Japan often means navigating tight-knit networks and long-term trust; in the US, it means moving fast, scaling big, and managing political risk in a system where security—and the industries that support it—still shape the rules of the game.

IMPLICATIONS FOR JAPAN

During the Cold War, the Japanese government was in lockstep with the US administration and therefore there was little room for Japanese companies to be all that engaged. It was not until the 1980s when an expectation arose that Japan needed to do things differently. Because of the rise of Japan's companies like Toyota that triggered a backlash with "Japan bashing" happening at that time, Japanese companies had to reorient and rethink their stories, investing and building out to show that, for example, more Toyota automobiles were being made in America than in Japan. Today, that level of complexity has reached another level. Now, companies must define and explain what values they represent.

Japan is at the top of the food chain for potential business opportunities and with a world increasingly focused on the East, many Americans are looking to Asia rather than Europe, especially given Japan's attraction both as a market and its cultural soft power. In response, Japanese companies are opening headquarters not just in financial centers such as New York but increasingly in places like Washington, DC, that will allow them to be closer to the regulatory environment.

STATE GOVERNMENT

For decades, Japan's approach to working with the United States has been heavily centered on Washington, DC, rooted in the belief that the most effective way to engage America is through the White House, Congress, and federal policymakers. This mindset, shaped by postwar diplomacy and the centrality of the US-Japan security alliance, often led Japanese officials and business leaders to overlook the broader complexity—and opportunity—of America's federal system.

Today, however, that perception is changing. Japanese companies, diplomats, and regional partners are increasingly recognizing the importance of engaging all fifty states, from governors and mayors to local chambers of commerce and community colleges. With decades of investment across the American heartland—from auto plants in Kentucky and Alabama to high-tech R&D centers in Texas and North Carolina—Japan is learning that the strength of its relationship with the US must be built not only in the corridors of Washington, but on the ground in communities where its presence has become integral to local economies and lives. This shift reflects a more mature and nuanced understanding of America—not as one voice in DC, but as a mosaic of interests, values, and partnerships that extend well beyond the Beltway.

LOBBYISTS AND ADVISORS

Another critical part of doing business in the US is the use of lobbyists and advisors. An advisor consults only on behalf of their client, but a lobbyist is hired to try to influence the passage of a law that will benefit another party. Lobbyists working on behalf of foreign entities in the US must be legally registered under the Foreign Agents Registration Act (FARA). In the US, even though legislative bills are submitted by members of Congress, many other government entities, like the White House, play a role in pushing (and even drafting) legislation.

In Japan, the vast majority of legislation is submitted by the government—specifically by the Cabinet—rather than by individual lawmakers, which stands in stark contrast to the US legislative process. This top-down structure reflects Japan's strong bureaucratic tradition, where elite ministries work closely with the ruling party to craft and refine policy before submitting it to the Diet for approval. As a result, laws are typically well-vetted and pass with fewer amendments. This fluid process is further solidified by the long-standing dominance of the LDP. In the United States, by contrast, legislation is introduced by individual members of Congress—often hundreds or thousands of bills per session—leading to a far more fragmented, partisan, and negotiation-heavy process. Whereas the US system is designed for debate and decentralization, Japan's model prioritizes stability and executive coherence, often giving bureaucrats and Cabinet officials more influence over legislative outcomes than backbench politicians.

THE BUSINESS OF LOBBYING

In Washington there is an entire private industry in business built up around executive power, executive privilege, and legislative bodies. Although lobbying often has a negative connotation in both the US and Japan, lobbyists function as an important part of the American legislative system and and are used by everyone from local governments to nonprofits to trade unions. They might, for example, provide a suggested text, saying that this would be the right thing for XYZ, and that the congressman should endorse it.

Lobbying in Nagatachō, Japan's political nerve center, operates quite differently from the often highly visible, well-funded, and adversarial lobbying culture found in Washington, DC. In Japan, lobbying is more discreet, relationship-based, and deeply embedded within long-standing networks between bureaucrats, industry groups, and politicians—particularly those within the ruling Liberal Democratic Party. Rather than relying on armies of professional lobbyists or flashy campaigns, Japanese interest groups—such as the Keidanren (Japan Business Federation), agricultural cooperatives, and sector-specific associations—tend to exert influence through quiet consultations, personal connections, and behind-the-scenes negotiations. Former bureaucrats often engage in *amakudari* ("descent from heaven"), taking positions in industries they once regulated, further blurring the lines between public and private sectors. In contrast, American lobbying is a highly formalized, billion-dollar industry characterized by registered lobbyists, political action committees (PACs), public advocacy, and rapid-response messaging campaigns. While both systems seek to influence policy, Japan's model is consensus-driven and rooted in long-term trust, whereas the American model is more transactional, competitive, and frequently public-facing.

Japanese businesses originally did not see lobbying as being in their purview as it was considered to be something done only by American citizens. But many Japanese companies also employ American citizens, so why shouldn't they avail themselves of the American way of doing business? Is it because lobbying has a negative connotation or that the Japanese don't want to be seen as tilting the scales from their very rules-based platform? Some Japanese companies are learning the hard way that they, too, are going to have to compete in the lobbying space by hiring lobbyists and competing themselves rather than relying on their government ministries that are having less and less success as recent negotiations on trade and tariffs have revealed in contrast to how the Nippon Steel case was settled.

In today's world, if you don't play in the lobbying system, your company is going to be the one that is negatively affected. In the past, Japanese hired lobbyists to provide intelligence but not to activate anything beyond that. Increasingly, Japanese companies are finding the need either to partner with American companies that are well-versed in lobbying in Washington and in state capitals or develop their own specialists in US government relations. This type of work, however, is not normal or practical in Japan where the focus is mostly on the financial and regulatory framework. In America, major businesses need to have government relations specialists just like they also need to have public relations specialists, something that the Japanese also have not been particularly adept at.

Japanese companies and government agencies have historically struggled with public relations and government relations in America due to a combination of cultural, structural, and linguistic factors. Rooted in a culture that values humility, discretion, and consensus over assertiveness and self-promotion, Japanese organizations often hesitate to proactively shape narratives or build visibility in the noisy, fast-paced American media and political environment. Unlike their American counterparts, who are accustomed to lobbying, messaging, and engaging multiple stakeholders across all levels of government, many Japanese firms have traditionally focused on Washington, DC, or operated behind the scenes, underestimating the importance of local engagement and public storytelling. Additionally, the lack of fluent English speakers with bicultural expertise in strategic communication has limited the ability to respond swiftly to crises or shape public perception. As a result, despite decades of investment and goodwill, Japan's presence in the US has often gone unnoticed or misunderstood—highlighting the need for a more dynamic, localized, and transparent approach to both public relations and government relations in today's interconnected, perception-driven world.

THE PRICE OF SUCCESS

To succeed in today's evolving, dynamic market, it is necessary for foreign businesses investing in the US to have a clearly defined and well-coordinated overall strategy. They must also interact with different areas of federal and state government. In Japan a CEO may feel that their main job is to take care of their company and sell its products or services, with America being seen as a static market. At this moment America is a dynamic, evolving partner with very different business practices than Japan. It is far messier to do business in America than it has ever been in the past. There are many fast-moving elements to understand and be aware of, including aspects of American history and culture that were not considered essential knowledge for doing business in the past.

Ultimately, if Japanese don't learn about America from an insider's perspective, they are not going to be successful in this new transactional system. The way Toyota is now operating with its full use of economic and social influence towards US business and political leadership demonstrates an insider's perspective. But many other Japanese companies do not. In a society like Japan, where exercising restraint is both expected and rewarded, this goes against all natural societal inclinations and means a sea change in attitudes and practices. At the core of what it means to be Japanese and to do business is building trusted relationships, not transactional ones, and to always consider that process for the future. Doing business in Japan is fundamentally about building long-term, trusted relationships rooted in mutual respect and shared commitment, whereas in America, business interactions tend to be more transactional, fast-moving, and focused on immediate results and contractual terms.

SUCCEEDING IN A TRANSACTIONAL SYSTEM

In the current and increasingly transactional American system, if you're holding something back or waiting for someone else to understand your needs without having to articulate them, you're going to be left behind. During the Cold War period, Japan had considerable success with a top-down route that relied heavily on the US government but also had strong business leadership and personalities like Akio Morita, the co-founder of Sony. Increasingly, Japanese companies and business leaders in the know have had to advocate for themselves, with or without their national counterparts and with or without their American counterparts, by going straight to the governors and mayors of local areas who welcome Japanese investment. Some of the greatest partnerships that we're seeing today are between the Japanese private sector and American state and local governments. Although those success stories don't get told very often, we should be talking about them openly and celebrating them in both America and Japan.

For anyone coming from a society like Japan's that prioritizes the needs of the other it can be very challenging to do business in America from an insider perspective. In fact, it goes against almost every natural instinct. The only way to accomplish this effectively is to be given permission to enter the "house" and actually to be invited inside America. That is where friends like Japan Society can help by becoming connectors for US-Japan beyond just a platform. Japan Society will never act as a lobbyist, but it is here to facilitate the understanding and goodwill needed for Japanese companies to make the trusted relationships that will allow them to succeed in America under the Trump administration. Advocacy and getting engaged in American democracy is no longer a "nice to have," but a "must have." Masayoshi Son has shown this in his leadership of Softbank in Japan and Elon Musk exemplified this interconnectedness through his special (albeit doomed) relationship with President Trump—and we're now seeing ramifications of that fallout. Japan must adapt to the new geopolitical environment that America has created on a multitude of levels. Above all, Japan should not be afraid to be an insider in America.

CHAPTER FOURTEEN

THE GEOPOLITICS OF *OMOTENASHI*

Omotenashi is a uniquely Japanese concept that goes beyond simple hospitality to connote a deep, almost intuitive attentiveness to the needs of others. Rooted in the cultural values of humility, respect, and service, *omotenashi* involves anticipating a guest's desires before they are expressed and offering care without expecting anything in return. It's not transactional but heartfelt—an unspoken contract of trust and grace between host and guest. From tea ceremony to customer service and even public infrastructure, *omotenashi* reflects Japan's commitment to thoughtfulness, harmony, and the dignity of shared human experience.

How do geopolitics and *omotenashi* intersect and how do these two apparent opposites work together for Japan and for US-Japan? In geopolitics, you always have to anticipate the worst from your opponent, using your own national interest as a guidepost. You must be prepared to fight for your rights and needs from a place where you are constantly one step behind and only one cycle away from disaster.

Omotenashi—anticipating the needs of the guest or the other, including another nation—is literally the opposite of geopolitics. A guest should never have to worry about their own needs because their host is always one step ahead in fulfilling them.

WHO BENEFITS?

The current focus on "America First" is nothing new. It's something that America and many nations have done for a long time, just not as overtly. In any given situation, it's not polite to say, "I'm only going to help you if it helps me." It sounds a lot better, particularly coming after a world war, to say, "We have shared interests and shared values." The Japanese are very good at doing this. Japan knows that for someone else to have a good experience they first need to understand the interests of the other. That's exactly what geopolitics should be about.

Of course, there are a lot more variants. When there are major disruptions and changes in the global system, in the absence of an agreed-upon framework of governance everyone gravitates toward the rule of the jungle. Whether it is a transition from a system of kingdoms and empires to nation states, or whether nations are trying to understand whether they want to become part of something multilateral like the United Nations, or something supranational, such as the European Union, the source of the disruption ultimately doesn't matter, it's the underlying national interests and responding to the external environment that drives change.

In the case of Japan and the US there has never really been that level of shock therapy but there have been major changes in mindset. World War II is the most obvious example. Ultimately, Japan embraced and internalized its defeat in a way that let America take the lead on everything, most noticeably in security. American forces provided the Japanese archipelago with a nuclear umbrella so that nobody could attack Japan, because an attack on Japan would be an attack on the United States—as explicitly stated in the 1951 Treaty of San Francisco and then spelled out in the 1960 version of the US–Japan Treaty of Mutual Cooperation and Security. On the US side, there's no such law. America's power and its capacity for deterrence is based purely on its own ability to strike back though a series of alliances—most notably the North Atlantic Treaty Organization and the US-Japan alliance—that networked the world together through Washington. During the Cold War, the concept of mutually assured destruction led to the logic that even if the Soviet Union had more nuclear warheads, America would make it so costly and painful that Russia would never dare to attack the United States.

That rules-based international order no longer exists today because warfare is being conducted by more than just military officials and national units. Contemporary geopolitical actors include technology companies, hackers, and terrorists with no loyalty to any national unity beyond their ideological viewpoints. It is very challenging to protect any society against the possibility that a person is willing to die for their cause, as America saw with the 9/11 attacks.

It is impossible to anticipate the needs of each person in the world or every single nation, but it is possible to identify common denominators. Following World War II, Japan's most important common denominator and its most important ally and security provider has always been the United States. As America becomes less interested in the global role it has played after the war, Japan is going to struggle to figure out how to put its needs first—because Japan has always assumed that its needs are one and the same with America's national interests. While that sometimes might have diverged on the margins, it has been consistent in East Asia. Japanese business leaders need to question what America is doing now, not only at the government level but also in the private sector.

Today, when Japanese question America, their attitude reflects a quiet but growing recognition that Tokyo must chart its own course—one that may align with, but is no longer bound to, Washington's. After all, Japan's national interests are increasingly diverging from US policy in key areas like China, trade, and defense autonomy. With regard to these areas, it is already becoming more up to business leaders rather than political leaders to negotiate the terms of agreement. Geopolitics only makes this more challenging. Today's world is much more complex, requiring layers of analysis beyond just nation-states to account for companies, individuals, and groups without a direct link other than ideology or extremism.

HARD VS. SOFT POWER

The concept of hard power versus soft power has been very important in my own thinking and experience as a political scientist. Joseph Nye, University Distinguished Service Professor Emeritus, and former dean of the John F. Kennedy School of Government at Harvard University first coined the term "soft power" in the late 1980s, popularizing the term in *Bound to Lead: The Changing Nature of American Power* (1990) and developing it further in *Soft Power: The Means to Success in World Politics* (2004). Professor Nye was a longtime friend of Japan, and I can't help but think that his own definitions of hard and soft power were in some ways influenced by Japan.

Hard power is basically defined as military power and often includes economic power. Usually, hard power is seen as a stick and soft power as a carrot. For example, during President Theodore Roosevelt's successful negotiation to end the Russo-Japanese War in 1905, he held out a stick to the Russians, saying that if they didn't make peace then, not only would Japan continue to take more territory but America would back Japan. To Japan, he offered the carrot of being seen as a rising power and invited Japan to the US to sign a vital peace treaty.

Soft power—the ability to shape the preferences and influence the behavior of others through attraction rather than coercion—is difficult to define and measure because it operates subtly, often becoming most visible in the absence of hard power like military force or economic sanctions. It draws on a nation's culture, values, institutions, and foreign policy credibility to inspire admiration or alignment. In Japan's case, soft power has been especially significant, as the country has constitutionally constrained its hard power capabilities since World War II. From anime and cuisine to technology, diplomacy, and societal discipline, Japan has cultivated a global image that exerts quiet influence without threat. This makes Japan a prime example of how soft power can serve as a nation's most enduring form of strength, particularly when traditional forms of power are limited or purposefully restrained.

It's not that anything which is not hard power is soft power by default. The use of military force as hard power is relatively easy to define, but how does the role between cyber security and offensive capabilities enter into the equation? In soft power, if you include certain economic metrics, couldn't you say that people are influenced by the investment strategies of some Japanese companies or the soft power appeal of culture such as video games and anime? From a historical point of view, hard power versus soft power worked very well in a Cold War context where the Soviet Union was effectively an empire behind the Iron Curtain where nobody did anything without Moscow's direct and explicit consent. On the American side it was empire by invitation, as Europe needed American bases to help protect against the Soviet Union, but this was also a case of soft power through influence. On the Japanese side after the war, General MacArthur realized that there was an opportunity to use American soft power in tandem with hard power by leaving the emperor in place and taking advantage of the imperial system to get what America needed—a strong Japan that could defend against the communist threat coming from Russia and, later on, from China. That is an example not only of soft power but also of the intersection of geopolitics and *omotenashi*.

OMOTENASHI AS A TACTIC

Looking further at how *omotenashi* can be used as a tactic, let's revisit the February 7, 2025, meeting between President Trump and Prime Minister Ishiba. Prime Minister Ishiba spent more than thirty hours preparing for that meeting, the equivalent of 10,000 hours in the bureaucracy. And that didn't even include flying time to the US. Staffers developed scenarios to prepare how Ishiba would respond to what President Trump might or might not say, and how he would need to respond in a meeting where all of the conversation would take place through an interpreter. The strategy was to come in with some significant wins for the president, otherwise he wouldn't feel good about the meeting. The Japanese came prepared to negotiate and also to try to satisfy some of the concerns that President Trump has had historically about the trade deficit. With Japan being the largest foreign investor in America, that meant identifying where that investment was needed most in terms of energy, infrastructure, technology and more, and making sure that whatever happened optically in the meeting could be managed beyond that one meeting.

For any world leader, the most difficult aspect of a meeting in the Oval Office is when it is held in front of the press. An official meeting can generally be controlled by both sides setting an agenda and a negotiated readout afterwards, but it becomes much more fluid when the president has his own way of doing things on livestream. During the February 7 meeting, Prime Minister Ishiba nodded as President

Trump spoke. To an American audience, Ishiba's nods meant that he was hearing and responding positively to what Trump was saying. From a Japanese point of view, Ishiba didn't give away any of his negotiating position, because in Japan you can agree by nodding your head without necessarily agreeing exactly with the point of view being articulated. In that meeting Japan knew that to avoid conflict it was best not to contradict the president. But Japan also knew that the conversation needed to be steered into a zone where one could agree to disagree.

Prime Minister Ishiba's February 7 visit with President Trump was broadly deemed a success, yielding several key outcomes: They reaffirmed the US-Japan alliance as the cornerstone of IndoPacific security, agreed to let finance ministers manage exchangerate issues, secured Japan's commitment to invest more in—nearly $1 trillion—and purchase additional US liquified natural gas (LNG), and agreed to move Nippon Steel's acquisition into a US-based investment. President Trump praised Japan's defense strengthening, and the two heralded a "new golden age" in bilateral ties—all without straining Japan on defense spending or trade deficits. Japan's initial success at the February 7 meeting was a moment of cultural *omotenashi* as a tactic, achieved through a careful balance of anticipation and hard preparation. Even the scheduling of the meeting on a Friday afternoon sandwiched in-between Israel and India's prime ministers, where more contentious and hot button issues were discussed, played to Japan's favor.

Unlike President Trump's meeting with Ukrainian President Volodymyr Zelenskyy, which ended in a shouting match with Vice President Vance, Japan's extensive preparation paid off. By anticipating what the president's opening salvo would be and what he might want in return, Prime Minister Ishiba was able to steer the conversation in a positive direction without arguing specific points. This was not only a considerable face saving for Japan, but Ishiba came out of the meeting with a clear mandate from the president of the United States that he was a worthy interlocutor, basically guaranteeing that he would stay in office as Japan's prime minister at that time.

Another interesting thing to note about the meeting is that it was interpreted by the same person who had previously interpreted for Trump's good friend Shinzo Abe, providing a personal point of connection through what was a very smart move by the Japanese bureaucrats. Additionally, Shinzo Abe's widow, Akie Abe, was the first Japanese national to meet with Trump after he won the presidential election, visiting him in Mar-a-Lago to remind him of the warm relationship between Trump and Abe and of the importance of US-Japan. Her meeting with President Trump set the stage for Prime Minister Ishiba's own meeting and helped the Japanese bureaucracy prepare for it.

THE HONORED GUEST

Omotenashi in Japanese culture is very much about anticipating the needs of one's guest. The visitor is greeted at the *genkan,* where they remove their shoes and put on slippers that are offered to them. Even the act of replacing someone's shoes with slippers is far beyond what we experience in America, where you walk directly into most houses and unless someone is bringing in a lot of mud on their feet, their shoes often stay on. In Japan, the host offers the slippers to their guest, and the guest receives the slippers from their host. Next, the guest is directed to where they will sit, an indication of where one stands in Japanese culture as well as within the family, something that is pretty common across Asia. Americans could definitely learn from these practices, because sometimes we make assumptions based on the strength of someone's personality or a lack of clear hierarchy in a particular situation.

There is a difference between *omotenashi* in the individual sense and how *omotenashi* translates into geopolitics. One way to consider this is to examine Japan's inherent pacifism. For the last eighty years Japan has had to learn how to interact with the world independent of military power, which has been a blessing in disguise. Japan does not have the ability to threaten countries like it used to, because its military has been subsumed and put on a lower footing. The Ministry of Foreign Affairs and the Ministry of Finance are the top ministries in Japan, and The Ministry of Defense became a ministry less than a decade ago. In the US, the Department of State and the Department of Defense are constantly calling each other out over resources. There is very little such dialogue in Japan, because the Ministry of Defense is less present at this type of conversation.

Then, there's another type of *omotenashi* —that is the use of soft power on a national level.

CHAPTER FIFTEEN

THE SOFT POWER OF A NATION

Where is soft power put to the test? Certainly the Olympics comes to mind. That's where every country is able to be proud of and excited about their athletes, with no hard power anywhere to be seen. Another setting that is well known in Japan, particularly in 2026, is the World Expo, when every four years the entire world comes together to pitch their country, culture, and civilization.

KAZAKHSTAN

The US hasn't been as actively engaged in the World's Fairs as other countries have been, but it has certainly been present at every Expo, including the World Expo in Kazakhstan that I had the privilege of running in 2017. Now Kazakhstan is a country that many Americans cannot find on a map, so what better place is there to consider in terms of the negative impact of soft power? Unfortunately, most Americans and many Westerners associate Kazakhstan with the film *Borat*, a fictional comedy about a hapless journalist from Kazakhstan that was actually filmed in Romania.

Because of *Borat*, Kazakhstan went through a national fiasco of trying to understand how they presented themselves to the world, because what they are most proud of—their nomadic culture, yurts, horses, and archery—is something that most Americans actually associate with Mongolia. *Omotenashi*'s dark side certainly showed up when *Borat's* Sacha Baron Cohen, who knew nothing about Kazakhstan, played off their national stereotypes in the most negative ways possible. The people of Kazakhstan then had to shed their undeserved reputation and show the world that they were not just an oil-rich, energy-dependent post-Soviet Union nation, but that they were located in one of the most strategic areas of the entire world—the middle or buckle of China's Belt and Road Initiative in Central Asia.

2017 WORLD EXPO

How America showed up at the 2017 World Expo in Kazakhstan is an interesting story. I had left the State Department and joined APCO Worldwide, a strategic communications company founded by Margery Kraus, whom I had come to know through my previous work for the government. When I was hired, Margery said euphemistically that I was going to be advising their international affairs department and that I would be helping the company and their clients think about the world. Very quickly I found myself interacting with a lot of world leaders such as New Mexico Governor Bill Richardson and Ambassador Tim Roemer, the former congressman from Indiana who was appointed ambassador to India under President Obama. I was tasked with finding ways of helping clients who didn't depend on federal lobbying.

Kazakhstan approached APCO with a major problem—the US government had no money designated to fund the American Pavilion at the 2017 Expo. Without America's presence in Kazakhstan the Expo was going to be a huge embarrassment for everyone because Russia would have the biggest pavilion on one side of the street with China on the other side, and a prime space had already been chosen for the USA Pavilion. Coordinating with the State Department that was supportive but didn't have any funds, APCO began conversations with major American companies that had significant equity in Kazakhstan, such as ExxonMobil, Coca-Cola, Citi, and Microsoft. They agreed to champion private sector funding for a USA Pavilion, but there was still a need for leadership from someone who was experienced with the American bureaucracy and a structure to support the USA Pavilion. That's how I ended up setting up a new nonprofit and becoming president and CEO of the USA Pavilion at the 2017 Expo in Kazakhstan in one of the most unusual but effective public-private partnerships I've ever had the privilege of leading.

USA PAVILION

By pulling together all of these pieces, Margery and I were able to create the USA Pavilion as a nonprofit public-private partnership. The biggest challenge was that this had all began in 2016 under the Obama administration, but the pavilion was set to open in the summer of 2017 under the incoming Trump administration, whose direction on energy policy was unknown. We pivoted very quickly from the Democrats to the Republicans, and I had a great experience working with Rick Perry, the US secretary of energy at that time and Kevin Cramer, a congressman from North Dakota who is now a senator. Ultimately everyone realized how important it was for America to show up. And because the bill was being footed by the private sector we were able to be as creative as we wanted to be. One of our biggest innovations was a student ambassador program, with sixty Americans from every state coming to spend the summer in Kazakhstan to welcome people coming to the USA Pavilion. I've always been very proud of being an American, and because I grew up in Japan as an outsider who constantly had to explain and show the best of America, it was easy for me to figure out how to show the best of America to visitors in Kazakhstan.

When people walked into the USA Pavilion for the first time, they found themselves in a dark theater where they were greeted by the best of America, experiencing everything from rodeo to country music alongside iconic moments and places in American history. After that presentation, they'd walk out outside to see what American companies like General Electric and Exxon had accomplished and what they were doing around the world, using Kazakhstan as a test case. At the very end of the pavilion we had two wings, like angel wings, one with the American flag and one with the Kazakh flag, and visitors could stand between them to be photographed and look like angels.

The USA Pavilion became one of the most popular spots to visit in the entire Expo. Even though we had a budget of around $10 million and, unofficially, the Russian and Chinese pavilions must have spent in the hundreds of millions, our pavilion was the most fun because we had our young student ambassadors to uplift visitors through American culture, music, and their boundless energy. Although America is not a major presence in Kazakhstan, where China is the largest investor financially and Russia the largest security player, the US private sector's reputation is among the most prestigious. For Expo 2017 we had a great partner in our commissioner general, Ambassador George Kroll, who was also the first American ambassador to build a Kazakh yurt in his backyard. Working with so many amazing people, especially our sixty student ambassadors, made it easy to tell America's story on a global stage.

Running the USA Pavilion in 2017 taught me that world's fairs are less about buildings than about promises—how a nation chooses to show up in the world. That lesson has come full circle with the USA Pavilion at Osaka's World EXPO 2025, whose popularity reflects a global appetite not just for American technology and culture, but for our openness and optimism. Serving on its advisory board across different administrations with our hardworking diplomats at the State Department and private sector partners was a privilege and a reminder that effective public diplomacy is a bipartisan relay, not a solo sprint. The baton we pass is continuity: welcoming visitors, convening partners, and telling a story big enough to include others. In Japan—where *omotenashi* meets American openness—the pavilion was a front porch to shared futures, a place where curiosity turned into collaboration. From the lessons of 2017 to the momentum of 2025, the constant has been the same: when America shows up—creatively, optimistically, and shoulder-to-shoulder—we are at our best.

ALL ROADS LEAD TO JAPAN

In many ways, running the USA Pavilion in Kazakhstan set me up on my journey toward leading Japan Society. But before that would happen, I joined Eurasia Group, a leading geopolitical risk consultancy. One of the things I gravitated toward there was Japan, which is Eurasia Group's second-largest market and I worked with Ian Bremmer, the company's founder and president, to create the first GZERO Summit in Tokyo. It was the largest geopolitical risk summit in the world, and I quickly found myself in direct contact with many high-level Japanese government and business leaders. When you have a summit like this it's natural to consider the world's biggest questions—what is going to happen between the two superpowers, the US and China? Then, you need to ask which other countries matter. Japan matters tremendously, and not in just a geographic sense. It became clear to me that Japan has so much to offer and that it wasn't just personal for me anymore, this was something that the entire world needed to understand. Unlike America, which has commodified and monetized the American Dream, Japan didn't have a strong projector of their soft power—yet.

From my perspective as a throughline leader at Japan Society, it has really only been in the last decade that we've seen the emergence of Japan in copying the American model, with Japan selling its own way of life and its own dream through its products. In the decades following World War II, Japan looked to the United States as a model for modernization and prosperity, embracing elements of the American Dream—from consumerism to industrial growth—as it rebuilt its society and economy. But today, Japan is no longer merely importing American dreams; it is exporting its own dreams. Through its products—whether minimalist Muji design, meticulous Toyota craftsmanship, or the aspirational lifestyles conveyed in anime, cuisine, and fashion—Japan is subtly promoting a distinctly Japanese way of life rooted in harmony, quality, and intentionality. This represents a quiet but powerful shift: Japan is no longer chasing someone else's narrative but crafting its own, offering the world a dream that values balance over excess, depth over speed, and community over individualism.

I would argue that Japan is even more successful at this than the US is, because the American Dream is, in many ways, more ubiquitous and even more driven by the "soft" side of things like education and innovation. Americans don't manufacture that many products anymore. We don't have the market on specific products like the Japanese do when it comes to anime, video games, cars, or watches, where Japan competes with the Europeans. In many ways, Americans are confused by Japan—they love Japanese products but wonder what Japan as a country can teach them. That's because the only thing that most Americans understand about Japan are its products and they don't know much at all about Japanese history and culture. As Americans we've sold the American Revolution, we've sold American democracy, and we've sold the American Dream. The Japanese don't show up in the world the same way that America does, with military forces and bases, with economic and trade packages, or development assistance. Japan usually just brings its soft power to the party. So where does Japan go from here?

Beyond its widely admired cultural exports, Japan offers the world deeper lessons in resilience, social cohesion, and the power of restraint. Its approach to governance, while often criticized for being slow-moving, demonstrates the value of consensus-building and long-term thinking in an era dominated by short-term gains. Japan's emphasis on public civility, cleanliness, and respect for shared spaces shows how individual responsibility can sustain collective well-being. In areas like disaster preparedness, elderly care, and public health, Japan leads not through bravado but through thoughtful design and systems that prioritize dignity and safety. Perhaps most importantly, Japan teaches that strength doesn't always come from assertiveness—it can come from quiet discipline, endurance, and the deep trust built through consistency over time.

FEELING THE MOMENT

It is clear that we are living through a significant period in time, one that is particularly dynamic. In the broader scope of the last 160 years of US-Japan history this moment is equivalent to the Meiji Restoration and Revolution or the period right after the end of World War II. This is different than the Vietnam War era or the Cold War period, and it is going to change the way that America and Japan see each other. Although American leadership shifts every four years with the presidential election cycle, the Japanese need to understand that their future is going to be shaped very differently, and this time it's not just by an external force over which they often feel that they have no control. That external force is not just the US president or the American states, it's a world that is looking for leadership and a new dream for the future.

We are in a moment when leadership is transitioning from an American-led order to a more multidimensional world, one in which the US dominates in the Western hemisphere but Eurasia is up for grabs. One way to look at this is to consider where the frictions are going to happen. In Asia, the obvious predominant power is China. But Asia is not only China—Asia is Japan, India, Korea, and the Association of Southeast Asian Nations (ASEAN). In that role, Japan no longer has the ability or the desire to predominate, but it wants and needs to be part of that new world order. If America is not fully committed to the US-Japan alliance in the way that it has been since the end of World War II, and the US is changing its position on global leadership, then Japan needs to make preparations for this shift now, especially if the US security guarantee is not as solid as before. Along with the nuclear umbrella, there are other elements to be considered regarding the footprint of American military forces in addition to the potential reorientation of American military power in general.

Japan is increasingly preparing for a world in which the US security guarantee, long seen as the bedrock of its postwar defense posture, may no longer be as ironclad as before. As the United States reevaluates its global leadership role and signals a more transactional or inward-looking approach, Japan has begun to quietly but steadily adjust. From doubling its defense budget and acquiring counterstrike capabilities to strengthening security partnerships with nations like Australia, India, and the UK, Japan is signaling a more proactive stance in regional security. At the same time, it is investing in emerging technologies, energy security, and economic resilience to reduce strategic dependence. This shift doesn't represent abandonment of the alliance but rather an evolution—Japan is hedging against uncertainty while stepping into a more autonomous role in shaping the Indo-Pacific order.

GLOBAL SHIFTS MEAN NATIONAL SHIFTS

The roles that Japanese influence and soft power have on Americans are changing. This is happening not just in America; it is taking place throughout the world. For example, the Saudi crown prince is absolutely fascinated by anime and is willing to do a lot of things for Japan because he has been influenced from an early age by the kind of Japanese culture that is not built into our Cold War models.

My own experience in the Middle East points to the enormous respect and resonance there is for Japan as a modern but not a Western country that can represent them and even the Global South whether at the G7 or the United Nations. Japanese culture resonates globally precisely because it offers a compelling alternative to Western norms—rooted not in dominance or expansion, but in refinement, restraint, and balance. This quiet strength appeals especially to regions like the Middle East and the Global South, where communities often seek models of development and modernity that preserve cultural identity rather than erase it. Japan's emphasis on humility, non-interventionism, and respect for tradition contrasts with more aggressive Western paradigms, making its approach more relatable and less threatening. Its success in marrying high technology with cultural continuity, and economic power with soft-spoken diplomacy, has inspired admiration across diverse societies navigating their own post-colonial or post-conflict paths. In this way, Japan projects a global relevance not through force, but through example.

COLLABORATION THROUGH SOFT POWER

There is an enormous space out there in the world for collaboration using Japan's soft power—its arts, culture, and history—to create areas for connection that are not geopolitically black and white. We don't know what the world will look like in ten years but these gray zones are becoming increasing important. The Japanese have to own their potential and make use of it because Japan is the only country that knows itself well enough to do this effectively.

Japan should more intentionally and strategically harness its culture and soft power by treating these assets not as static, but as active tools of diplomacy, influence, and economic engagement. Specifically, Japan should invest in cultural infrastructure abroad—expanding Japan houses, funding more Japanese language and arts education, and supporting local cultural festivals that highlight Japanese aesthetics, food, and values. It should empower a new generation of cultural ambassadors—not just officials, but chefs, designers, musicians, and animators—to represent Japan's modern identity globally. Japan should also integrate its cultural assets into its foreign policy, linking cultural exchange to development partnerships in the Global South and branding its technology and innovation exports through distinctly Japanese values of quality, harmony, and sustainability. This is precisely where Japan Society comes in—serving as a platform that connects Japan's cultural and intellectual capital with American and global audiences, building lasting relationships, fostering understanding, and helping Japan project soft power with purpose and impact.

As an outsider who has become an insider, I see this up close and personal. I want more Japanese to understand that, as we say in America, "sometimes you have to fake it until you make it." From its precision engineering and timeless aesthetics to its deep respect for tradition, social harmony, and innovation, Japan offers a blend of qualities that continue to amaze and inspire America and the world. Even if Japan isn't comfortable promoting itself on the global stage or saying that it is the best civilization in the world because of its past history, there are many things about Japan that are admirable and amazing, all of which the Japanese should be proud to showcase to the world. We must start these conversations now.

Both the government and the private sector need to work together to meet the challenge of leading Japan in this changing world. On the global stage Japan is often perceived as being weak because its mechanisms of power are very clearly divided. In Japan's current siloed approach political leaders focus on the political side, business leaders on the business side, and cultural leaders on the cultural side. All of these areas need to be brought together because no one sector is strong enough to have a disproportionate influence on the world. I'm not talking about having baseball superstar Shohei Ohtani run for prime minister, but for Japan to get behind how it is seen in the world and show up in that way. There are moments in Japanese history, whether with Tokugawa Ieyasu and the Tokugawa Shogunate or Prime Minister Shigeru Yoshida and the Yoshida Doctrine, where leaders found ways of turning weakness into strength or defining what shapes the character and civilization of Japan by looking within themselves to meet the world outside. The US is in a moment of self-doubt and crisis as we fight internally among ourselves to decide who gets to define and speak for America, but the same struggle is not taking place in Japan. It's never really happened that way—whoever speaks for Japan on the global stage is often different from who speak for Japan internally.

DEFINING JAPAN'S NATIONAL INTEREST

Even if the US-Japan alliance stays within the traditional bounds of the Cold War bilateral relationship, there are going to be some tough negotiations ahead. What happens if President Trump doesn't want to support the American military presence in Japan? The US-Japan Status of Forces Agreement (SOFA) stipulates the legal framework under which US military forces operate in Japan, outlining the rights and responsibilities of both countries, including jurisdiction over crimes, tax exemptions, base usage, and the movement and activities of US personnel stationed in Japan. Renegotiating any type of agreement between countries and bureaucracies like the US and Japan, especially the SOFA, is going to be difficult and will reopen old wounds from the past. My fundamental point is that if the international order as we know it is changing structurally, then whatever that bilateral context is will also need to adapt. The US president may be unwilling or unable to see this but that does not negate Japan's need to approach it in this way.

To put this in a broader context, the Japanese need to understand what this transaction might look like and how it might not have to define the whole like the US-Japan Treaty of Mutual Cooperation and Security. President Trump thinks of things very differently. He thinks that something can always be renegotiated or refinanced, very much like a real estate transaction. This is an opportunity for Japan to actually determine its own self-interest in the world, not just to have it defined by the US, as has happened for the past seventy years or more.

For Japan to be able to negotiate this type of deal it must first define its own national interest. For me, Japan's national interest could be defined as preserving peace and stability in the Indo-Pacific, ensuring energy and economic security, maintaining a rules-based international order, safeguarding territorial integrity, and sustaining a society that balances technological advancement with cultural continuity. I'm not convinced that Japan has been able to do that yet, not only because it hasn't been asked to, but because it hasn't been forced to. America's president is not going to ask Japan to define its national interest, but the Japanese themselves are going to be asked that question—and by their electorate. Japan needs to find an answer this critical question, and that answer that will become a kind of North Star to guide the country toward its long-term future.

A LOST MOMENT

The past can teach us to plan for the unexpected. Five years after the COVID pandemic, even at the moment of the Osaka World Expo, Japan is still feeling the effects of the pandemic. After the Tokyo Olympics were postponed, the following year limited spectators were permitted at outdoor events only, with a lot of important sports being minimalized. Many of the companies sponsoring the Olympics literally received no benefits. In a period of globalization, albeit a unique one, Japan's Olympics reinforced the opposite message—that Japan was going to stay closed longer than almost any other nation with the exception of China. That postponement had an enormous impact on Prime Minister Shinzo Abe, who had been the force behind bringing the Olympics to Japan. After the games were postponed, Abe stepped down and Yoshihide Suga, his chief cabinet secretary and deputy, took over the leadership of Japan.

Every Olympics has its great stories, but when I saw the Paris Olympics, that's what I wished the Tokyo Olympics had been—because it was made for a TV audience that showcased all the glory of France and its national icons. Japan didn't manage to present the best of itself at the Tokyo Olympics, even under the most difficult circumstances, and that had a huge impact on the Japanese psyche.

Japan's moment with the 2020 Olympics in Tokyo ultimately felt squandered. It was an opportunity to show case Japan's soft power to the world. Where a global showcase could have solidified its soft power, the 2020 Olympics instead became synonymous with logistical compromises, public discord, and diminished impact. Held amidst the COVID pandemic, events were largely staged behind closed doors in empty stadiums, dampening the celebratory atmosphere and disconnecting Tokyo from the world crowd. Further undermining the legacy were high-profile corruption scandals, bribery charges and questionable environmental decisions—from timber sourcing to asbestos concerns—that strongly tainted the narrative of a safe, sustainable Olympics.

In stark contrast, Paris 2024 was widely lauded for its vibrant public engagement, cultural elegance, and digital innovation—rooted in Art Deco design, open-air ceremonies on the Seine, and a record number of viewers—offering a template of successful legacy-building that Tokyo failed to grasp. China, though, used the pandemic as an excuse to showcase a very propaganda-heavy narrative of its rise as proof that it was on the upswing. In the 2022 Winter Olympics in China, we saw an example of the politicization of soft power. In the 2020 Japan Summer Olympics, we saw how missed opportunities can have a significant national impact. From all of this, it is clear that Japan needs to use its soft power on the global stage in conjunction with strong and dedicated leadership to ensure its future in a changing world.

CHAPTER SIXTEEN

KIZUNA: OPPORTUNITIES AND LESSONS LEARNED

Growing up as a missionary kid in Hokkaido, we'd come home from church and discuss the sermon over lunch as a family. We'd be talking about whatever lesson we should have learned, and my brother and I would literally roll our eyes in frustration, saying "Who cares what verse it was or who died?" Then my father would ask us, "What's the one golden nugget from today?" What he meant was, "What is the one thing you could take away and apply to your life today from that sermon?" There are golden nuggets in each of these chapters. I've tried to be intentional about what Japan can learn not only from its own history but by interacting with the US. We've now gone beyond the *genkan* for both America and Japan and explored the importance of insider/outsider perspectives and awareness for business as well as our own societies. Throughout the book we've unpacked the thematics, but in this chapter we'll take a hard look at how one crisis can define everything—and the urgency of addressing that crisis.

THE CURRENT CRISIS

The crisis today is bigger than just what's happening in America, although that's where it is at the most extreme. It's an unraveling of the last eighty years of postwar history. Our democracies, our economies, and our way of life as a globalized world are all at a crisis point. We sometimes talk about crisis in terms of history—it's a once-in-a-lifetime or once-in-a-generation crisis, or it's a 160-year, hundred-year, or an eighty-year crisis. Is this a forty-year crisis? Many of us originally believed where we are now was the apex of a forty-year crisis. That would take us back to the Vietnam War era and the Civil Rights Movement. But I think it's bigger than that. The reason I feel compelled to speak out now is not to offer an indictment of the current moment that we're living through but to show that it has taken us at least five years to get here. We're still unpacking what the COVID pandemic means to us and we're also still living through what 3.11 and 9/11 did to our respective countries.

We're feeling this moment most acutely because we are actually living it. Not since eighty years ago, at the end of World War II, has there been such a reshaping of an entire economic system and international order. The way that President Trump is presenting America as a leader by saying "America First" means that America will focus on itself and doesn't need to explain itself or its global impact. Many past leaders went to great lengths to state how putting America First was actually putting the world first at the same time. That veneer is now off in a new system that is far more transactional and short term. In many ways, this version of "America First" is also an emotional response to American populism, with people feeling that they have been betrayed and left behind by globalization, from which they have not personally benefited. I don't believe this because I have seen what the US-Japan relationship has accomplished in both Japan and America.

The US-Japan relationship has profoundly shaped both nations, transforming a postwar alliance into one of the most successful bilateral partnerships in modern history. In Japan, it enabled rapid economic recovery and modernization, underpinned by security guarantees that allowed the country to focus on industrial growth and social development. In the United States, the alliance secured a critical foothold in Asia, supporting American strategic interests while benefiting from Japan's technological innovation, stable investment, and cultural influence. Together, our two countries have fostered shared prosperity through trade, academic and cultural exchange, and joint leadership on global issues from climate to regional security. The relationship has not only stabilized the Indo-Pacific but also deepened mutual understanding, proving that former adversaries can become indispensable allies.

As we navigate an era marked by political polarization, waning trust in institutions, and shifting global power dynamics, the US-Japan relationship will need to evolve fundamentally beyond the traditional top-down framework that has long defined it. The old model—anchored in elite diplomacy between Washington and Tokyo—is no longer sufficient to meet the challenges of this moment. With leadership increasingly paralyzed or transactional, the burden is shifting to individual citizens, companies, and local actors to sustain and advance the alliance. Whether through people-to-people exchange, grassroots cultural diplomacy, or corporate investment and collaboration, the future of US-Japan ties will depend on broader networks of trust, creativity, and shared purpose. This more decentralized, dynamic model won't replace the strategic alliance—but it will ensure its resilience in a world where formal leadership too often falters.

What worries me most in this moment are the simplistic, reactive calls to put "America First" or build walls—whether literal, ideological, or economic. History has not been kind to wall-builders. Walls isolate populations, calcify fear, and ultimately crumble under the weight of their own limitations. In contrast, history remembers and rewards those who build bridges—between cultures, communities, and competing interests. In the US-Japan space, we need more bridge-builders—people and institutions willing to reach across divides, create shared understanding, and invest in long-term connection over short-term gain. The future of this alliance will not be secured by retreating inward, but by leaning forward—together.

Speaking on behalf of history, I will say that it is fine to be an insider, but if you build a wall to protect your position as an insider, and you are not able to travel easily between the inside and the outside of your wall by bridges joining the two spaces, that wall will ultimately hurt or destroy the people living on both sides. Getting around that wall means building people-to-people bridges, like those created by the US-Japan relationship. This is not a short-term process, and it's also not a transaction that can show an immediate benefit or profit. Bridge-building is about collaboration and human connection. It's also about global collaboration. When I look at my own life, I can see what Japan Society means to all those who value the US-Japan relationship. That's the microcosm of a much greater story, a story that can put Japan on the global stage, a story that needs to be told and celebrated before it's too late.

My own faith tradition teaches, "Blessed are the peacemakers," a reminder that those who seek to heal, unite, and reconcile are doing sacred work. I've long understood this to mean not just peacemakers in the diplomatic or religious sense, but bridge-builders—those who quietly labor to connect worlds, often without recognition or reward. This deeply resonates with Japanese culture, which reveres humility and celebrates the unsung heroes who work behind the scenes with quiet dedication. Whether it's a master craftsman, a lifelong public servant, or a teacher shaping young minds, Japan honors those who build, not boast. In both American faith and Japanese values, the message is clear: the future belongs to those who bring people together.

THE UNSUNG HEROES—JAPAN-AMERICA SOCIETIES AND SISTER CITIES

In an era of summits, sanctions, and shifting global power, diplomacy often looks like the domain of heads of state, corporate titans, and military alliances. Yet behind the grand gestures and treaty-signings, a quieter, steadier form of diplomacy has long bound the United States and Japan together—not through strategy, but through people. This is the realm of the Japan-America Societies and sister cities partnerships, the underappreciated but indispensable human infrastructure of the US-Japan alliance. They are the cultural translators, the hometown hosts, the student exchange organizers, the festival planners. They are the bridge-builders who remind both nations that what ultimately sustains international relationships is not ideology or interests, but relationships—the kind formed over shared meals, home stays, high school concerts, and decades of personal connection.

As the US and Japan navigate a rapidly changing global order—marked by rising authoritarianism, climate disruption, and technological competition—the role of these community-level institutions has never been more vital. They are the ballast keeping the bilateral ship steady, no matter which way the political winds blow.

POST-COVID EXCHANGE

Japan's border closure during COVID, among the strictest of any democratic nation as previously discussed, brought most in-person exchanges to a halt. The ripple effects were profound: high school exchange trips were canceled, tea ceremony lessons were suspended, local festivals were called off, and many grassroots organizations feared for their survival.

And yet, something unexpected happened. Groups began to experiment with digital diplomacy—virtual homestays, Zoom-enabled language classes, collaborative manga-drawing projects between students in Oregon and Okayama. These programs lacked the intimacy of physical presence, but they preserved and even widened access to Japan for rural schools and communities previously left out of such exchanges.

One standout story is the Torrance, California–Kashiwa, Chiba, sister city program. For nearly fifty years, it has brought together high school students in alternating summers. During COVID, the program went virtual but retained all its key elements—language immersion, cultural presentation, even shared cooking over Zoom. In 2023, it returned to in-person exchange, stronger than before—its alumni base having grown online during the pandemic.

THE MAGIC OF GRASSROOTS DIPLOMACY

These sister city programs don't often deal with sanctions or submarines. Instead, they work in something far more lasting—the memory of a homestay with a Japanese host family, a high school kendo match, a joint art project between elementary schools. These seemingly small moments become the foundation of lifelong connection—and sometimes even careers in diplomacy, business, or cultural leadership. They remind us that a real relationship between nations doesn't live in embassies alone. It lives in friendships formed over shared meals, karaoke duets, and awkward icebreakers that lead to something profound.

As we look toward the future of US-Japan relations, we must invest not just in treaties and trade, but in town halls and tea houses, in school visits and shared festivals, and in the young people who may one day lead but who today simply need the chance to know and be known by someone across the Pacific. If the "top of the bridge" is built by leaders and policies, then it is the grassroots exchanges that anchor the bridge on solid ground. And in a world of uncertainty, that grounding—the human kind—is more necessary than ever.

REAL LIVES, REAL BONDS

Ask a Japanese high school student who spent a summer in Spokane about their experience, or an American mayor who visited their sister city of Yamagata, or a Texas businesswoman whose company connected with a Kyoto partner through a local Japan-America Society event. These experiences are not footnotes to foreign policy—they are the foundation.

Standout examples are Japan-America Societies of Texas both in Dallas and Houston which have turned a region once peripheral to US-Asia engagement into a hub of cultural diplomacy and business connectivity. When the 2011 Great East Japan Earthquake struck, many American sister cities mobilized aid and comfort, not out of diplomatic obligation, but because they had friends in those towns. Some sent funds; others sent letters of encouragement. In a moment of crisis, it wasn't just the Pentagon or State Department that first responded—it was the Japan Society in New York and friends across the country writing to our communities with offers of help. It was citizens reaching across the Pacific to say: "We're with you."

As generational shifts and digital connectivity reshape how young people experience the world, Japan-America Societies and sister cities are evolving, too. While defense alliances and trade negotiations will always dominate headlines, the Japan-America Societies and sister cities operate not in embassies, but in school auditoriums and city halls. They don't issue communiqués—they issue invitations. And in doing so, they ensure that the US-Japan relationship is not just strategic—it's personal.

In the face of geopolitical uncertainty and shifting public sentiment, Japan and America can look to these local institutions as models of what durable diplomacy looks like. Not quick fixes or grand gestures, but quiet persistence, rooted in friendship and mutual respect. They are our unsung heroes.

JAPAN'S SOFT POWER AND THE FUTURE OF US -JAPAN RELATIONS

If you close your eyes and imagine a face for Japan, chances are it isn't a prime minister or a business leader. It's not a flag or even Mount Fuji. It's a character—a little yellow Pokémon, a red-capped plumber, a wide-eyed ninja, or a mouthless cat with a pink bow. From Hello Kitty to *Super Mario*, from Pikachu to Naruto, Japan's most enduring global ambassadors don't carry passports—they carry nostalgia, magic, and joy. And while diplomats and executives often focus on security alliances or trade pacts, they often miss what may be Japan's most potent global currency: its soft power—shaped by anime, video games, and the broader "content industry."

To some, names like *Dragon Ball*, *Naruto*, *Sailor Moon*, or even *Demon Slayer* may already feel cliché—cultural artifacts from childhood or over-merchandised phenomena. But that's precisely the point: these works have become cliché because they're universally known. That universality is not trivial—it's transformative. When a kid in Kansas, Kyoto, or Kayseri can name the same characters, mimic the same hand signs, or collect the same cards, we are witnessing the true nature of global cultural influence. Japan's characters aren't just entertainment—they are connective tissue for a generation raised on shared symbols. And they are part of a larger architecture of trust, curiosity, and creative admiration between the US and Japan.

THE BUSINESS OF SOFT POWER

Japan's content industries are more than cute mascots and million-unit games. They are economic powerhouses. In 2022 alone, the global anime market surpassed $26 billion, and Japan's video game industry—names like Nintendo, Sony, Capcom, and Bandai Namco—continues to shape global gaming culture. Yet it's not just about sales—it's about the values these stories export: friendship, perseverance, teamwork, respect for nature and tradition, and the idea that power comes not from domination, but from self-mastery and compassion.

These values, encoded into Japan's soft power exports, often contrast with Western media tropes and provide a refreshing narrative that resonates across cultures. That cultural contrast is what makes the US-Japan partnership so fruitful: a synthesis of storytelling styles, design philosophies, and even moral frameworks.

AMERICA—THE SOFT POWER AMPLIFIER

Japan may create, but America amplifies. The two countries have built an unspoken pipeline of cultural co-creation—from Hollywood adaptations to English dubs, fan conventions to cosplay meetups. Without America's vast media infrastructure and enthusiastic fanbase, many of Japan's most iconic soft power exports may never have gone global.

Think of how Netflix has become a platform for anime. How Comic Con in San Diego now has Japanese pavilions or Anime NYC has mainstreamed *otaku* culture here in New York. Or how *Pokémon GO*—a joint venture between Japan's Nintendo and America's

Niantic—turned city parks into playgrounds for the international digital community. Japan's soft power is often reduced to *kawaii* (cuteness), but its appeal is far deeper. There's the quiet resilience of Studio Ghibli, the philosophical undertones of games like *Zelda*, and the intergenerational loyalty of franchises like *Final Fantasy*. These are not simply distractions—they are emotional languages.

The US-Japan alliance is strengthened every time a child learns Japanese to understand anime in its original language, or when gamers collaborate across borders in co-op missions. It is bolstered by teachers using manga to teach literature, and by artists drawing inspiration from Kyoto's brushstrokes and Akihabara's neon dreams.

THE STRATEGIC VALUE OF STORYTELLING

In a time when democracy is contested, truth is fragmented, and anxiety looms large, Japan's soft power offers something rare—hopeful imagination. Its stories invite us to believe that the small can overcome the mighty, that tradition and technology can coexist, and that friendship—however unlikely—can save the world. Soft power doesn't show up in treaty negotiations or press briefings. It shows up in lunchboxes, YouTube playlists, and fan art. It's not a replacement for hard power—but it is the human architecture that sustains alliances long after the headlines fade.

To fully understand the potential of US-Japan relations, we must look beyond the *genkan*—the polite entryway of formal diplomacy—and step into the deeper, often messier living room of shared cultural life. That's where you'll find a kid in Brooklyn sketching Naruto, a college student in Tokyo studying American film, or a global CEO reflecting on Miyamoto's game design philosophy. These aren't fringe experiences. They are the new center. They are the future. And Japan's soft power—once underestimated—is now undeniable. The question isn't whether Hello Kitty or Pikachu are "too familiar." The question is whether we've been paying close enough attention to what they've already achieved—and what more they can inspire for cultural diplomacy at a time when leadership is in crisis.

CHAPTER SEVENTEEN

CITIZENSHIP AND LEADERSHIP

A crisis of leadership occurs when there is no leader or institution that everyone can believe in.

Americans used to believe in media; the military used to be apolitical; the Supreme Court has become overtly political. All of these have now been weaponized. We have little left to guide us in determining who should be our local leaders, or even how to come to terms with our current national leader. Even if you are a great showman, when you start lying to the world, your word cannot be taken at face value. That is a real problem, particularly for a country like Japan that values honor, respect, and social good. I'm a firm believer in America and American democracy but we are going through a difficult period where there is going to be a lot of internal focus and discussion. Our political elites have not done a good job of educating Americans on the importance of globalization and international relations, whereas in Japan, the importance of the US and global history has been reinforced since the end of World War II with little discussions of what a plan B or Japan's own leadership role independent of the US should look like.

JAPAN AS A GLOBAL LEADER

It is critical for Japan to actively and openly debate its own role as a global leader—independent of the United States—not out of disloyalty to the alliance, but out of recognition that nations have permanent interests, not permanent alliances. While full decoupling from the US is neither realistic nor desirable today, Japan must develop a clearer strategic identity rooted in its own values, capabilities, and geographic realities. As the international order becomes more fragmented and power shifts toward multipolarity, Japan can no longer afford to rely solely on Washington's direction. Whether in setting standards for AI governance, leading climate diplomacy, or stabilizing the Indo-Pacific, Japan has the credibility, resources, and moral authority to lead in its own right. But leadership begins at home—with the courage to question assumptions and chart a future that serves Japan's long-term national interests, even when those diverge from traditional partners.

Japan should now step up as a leading voice of the free world—not just as a substitute when America retreats, as it did when Prime Minister Abe salvaged the Trans-Pacific Partnership, but as a proactive, values-driven leader charting its own course. This time, however, Japan's leadership must be more holistic—a whole-of-society approach that draws not only from government policy but also from the strength of its corporations, universities, cultural institutions, and civil society. Japan's natural strengths as a soft power leader—its global reputation for quality, trust, and restraint—position it uniquely to lead in areas like technology ethics, sustainable development, and peacebuilding. In a world searching for stability and thoughtful leadership, Japan doesn't need to mimic American power; it needs to amplify its own, in a distinctly Japanese way that bridges East and West, and inspires a new kind of global cooperation rooted in quiet strength and collective responsibility.

BEYOND THE AMERICAN WAY

Meanwhile Americans need to move beyond the reflexive belief that leadership always means going first or doing things the American way. In an increasingly interconnected and complex world, humility is not weakness—it's wisdom. There are multiple ways to solve problems, build societies, and lead on the global stage, and many of them don't originate in Washington. From Japan's consensus-driven approach to policymaking to the Nordic emphasis on social trust or the African prioritization of community, different models offer valuable lessons. America doesn't have to lead every time, everywhere; sometimes the most powerful leadership is listening, learning, and supporting others who are better positioned to lead in specific contexts. True leadership means recognizing that others have something to teach—and having the confidence to follow when the moment calls for it.

It's not only our leaders who need to take responsibility for their actions. The lesson of the American experience and American democracy is that the most powerful title we all carry as individual Americans is that of "citizen." Being a citizen is the greatest responsibility of any person in a democracy. It's not just voting or being civically engaged that matters, it's everything you do—from the way you raise your family to the way you determine your profession, to the choices you make as a consumer. In the US, we, as citizens, are ultimately responsible for the leaders whom we elect to represent us. That's not quite the same in Japan, where the responsibilities of leaders and citizens are understood implicitly through the filters of a homogeneous society. America's messy social contract, on the other hand, is an accurate reflection of both our diversity and our abundance as a nation. But when the world becomes particularly dark and chaotic, a sense of inner peace and well-being is needed, now more than ever. That is where Japan can be there for America, not to make our decisions for us but to create a space that can bring people together even as we struggle with our deeply divided society.

Japan can be there for America not by dictating solutions or assuming the role of fixer, but by offering something increasingly rare in our deeply divided society: a space of calm, reflection, and respectful dialogue. This space need not be physical—though it could take the form of cultural centers, joint forums, or university partnerships—it is above all a conceptual and relational space where complexity is honored over polarization, and listening is valued as much as speaking. Imagine a place where American and Japanese thinkers, artists, business leaders, and citizens come together not to win debates, but to understand perspectives—through shared meals, cultural exchange, collaborative problem-solving, and even silence. Rooted in the Japanese ethos of harmony (*wa*) and patience, this space can offer Americans a model of engagement that slows down the rush to judgment and opens up the possibility of connection. At a time when our national conversation often feels like shouting past one another, Japan could help America rediscover the dignity of dialogue whether over a bowl of tea or simply through intentional mindfulness.

THE MINDSET OF A GLOBAL CITIZEN

We've talked a lot about insider and outsider perspectives. Growing up as an American in Japan, I had to figure out who I was. I asked myself, "If I'm American, then why am I in Japan? And if I'm Japanese, then why do I look different from everyone else?" The way I solved this was by adopting the mindset of a global citizen, which does not prevent me from being an American citizen or from actively exercising my role as such. Being a global citizen adds a layer—the understanding that we live in a global community. Yet for a citizen of any country who has never left their homeland, it is difficult to understand what it means to live in an interconnected way. Many Japanese don't fully appreciate their homeland until they leave Japan. I've had the privilege from a very young age of seeing America from the outside. To me, being a global citizen is to be patriotic and proud of your homeland and your country. It means knowing that there are many different opportunities and diverse ways of doing things that can benefit everyone. For me, there is no one right way of doing everything. For individuals and countries alike there are ways that work better at different times or in different seasons. Global citizens, to my mind, are always looking for opportunities to connect with others and to bring in experiences from the outside.

By necessity, all leaders have to be insiders who are as well-informed as outsiders but, as with being a citizen, being a leader is also a two-way street. When I talk about being an insider or an outsider, it's an acknowledgment that so much of what people follow and want to do is in relationship with a leader. A leader needs to have a deep understanding of what makes people tick, from the national, local, and community levels to the environment, including historic narratives and stories all the way through to knowing what drives our personal identities as citizens. A leader becomes familiar with all of this through experience but at the same time, they can become too engrained in local matters. Whether they are a mayor, a governor, or a president, as someone who represents all of those people a leader needs to be able to take a step back and understand the bigger picture. At the end of the day, there's a lot that connects us as human beings, whether as Americans or Japanese, or as New Yorkers, Floridians, or Virginians, and that connection is ultimately what allows us to have a conversation as human beings.

VALUING JAPAN

For a Japanese business leader, understanding what drives America is key. However, America and being an American is not just one thing, it's a multitude of things. Within a short geographic radius in the US there are many different identities. There are certain things that unite us, and these are connected to our national narrative. Today, as our national institutions are being politicized and weaponized in partisan ways, doing business in America has become even more fraught and because it is now impossible to stay above or outside of politics, it's necessary to become part of it. It's necessary to be in that process not as an American but as someone who understands what motivates the decision-making of American leaders at all levels from state to national. At the same time, by understanding how America works it is also possible to see what Japan has to offer to the world beyond just aligning with American strategic leadership.

Japan cannot realize how much it has to offer the world until it is able to see itself from the outside. Many Japanese don't fully realize how unique they are as an ancient civilization rooted in harmony, partly because their cultural instinct is to blend in rather than stand out—what feels normal and unremarkable to them, like centuries of ritualized coexistence and social cohesion, is in fact extraordinary to much of the world, which often struggles to achieve that kind of balance. When a person leaves their homeland, in that moment, they discover something that they've always had that is a part of who they are, which is a deep sense of longing—because human beings have to be connected to something that is greater than themselves. While we can be incredibly selfish and focused on survival, we are also communal. What Japan offers is a strong, steady self-confidence that has in some ways manifested itself on the global stage as being very humble and declaring that it has nothing to offer the world. As we get further and further away from American dominance in all senses of the word, the soft power that brings us together, both defining us and making us human, becomes even more attractive. Japan has a far longer history of dealing with the transition from hard power to having value in the world—that's value because of what Japan is, which is soft power.

IT'S A GLOBAL WORLD

In the twenty-first century, the likelihood of a country like Japan being able to cut itself off from the rest of the world as it did during the Tokugawa period is practically zero. Exceptions include North Korea and perhaps Iran or Cuba. But Japan already made the choice not to withdraw by default, when it was forcibly opened to the world by the US 160 years ago. Although it's impossible to go back in time physically, one can go back in time mentally. Ironically enough that is what the US is going through now in terms of rebuilding a world of tariffs and domestic manufacturing to try to recreate the supposed glory days of what made America great. This mental time travel is something that America is currently struggling with. I don't think Japan has the same problem, but the instincts of the Japanese people to look only internally and not to consider any global implications have certainly been reinforced by the COVID pandemic. My hope is that Japan will learn from some of its mistakes after COVID and understand that its unique value proposition is very much its own social harmony and ancient civilization, alongside its soft power. Although this value proposition has been modernized, it hasn't fully been Westernized, and that's always been Japan's appeal.

In a global world that is interconnected and increasingly less about location, Japan has something very special to offer the world—a deeply engrained philosophy of harmony, precision, and quiet resilience that stems from its history and culture, not its geography, and which manifests in everything from design and diplomacy to human relationships and problem-solving. What's stopping Japan from making full use of its unique value proposition? It's simplistic but true to say that Americans are more extroverted, confident, and willing to stand on the global stage while Japanese are humbler and hold themselves back.

The norms of Japanese society make it possible to live together very closely. After World War II, Japan was prevented by its constitution from going beyond its own islands. But we're talking about expanding philosophically what is Japanese that isn't physical. What if in this way Japan can be invited "into" a country that wants Japanese content and Japanese ways of doing things from cars to watches, and from food to architecture? Rather than being passive and saying that it has nothing to contribute to the world, Japan needs translate its culture so it becomes universal. Going from national to universal is something that America did very well during its rise to prominence in terms of making the American Dream global. I don't think that the Japanese Dream has ever been global. The Japanese Dream—characterized by stability, harmony, craftsmanship, and community well-being over individual excess—offers a quieter, more sustainable vision of success that may be more appealing to a world increasingly disillusioned with the hyper-competition and inequality often associated with the American Dream. What I would wish for Japan, and what I hope for Japanese companies and individuals, is that they are not too narrowly constrained by the straitjacket of what the America Dream used to represent, because in the twenty-first century the Japanese Dream should be universal and deeply appealing, perhaps even more so than the American Dream.

A CALL TO ACTION

We're now looking at the twenty-first century, both in terms of how we view democracy and how we do business nationally and internationally.

What I've learned from a political science perspective in international relations is that it takes a long time to go from one order to another. The bipolar world created by America as the leader of the "free world" since the end of World War II, which Japan has very much been a part of, has dragged on for at least twenty years since the end of the twentieth century. Changes that began with the 9/11 attacks are now being experienced in terms of a transitioning global economic system, a system that is being reordered and reshaped by tariffs as well as by relations between nations. We need to take a look at the past and learn from the lessons of history.

I wish I could go back to the Roaring Twenties and warn people that all their extravagance would all come to an end with the Great Depression, leading to the most terrible war that humans have ever fought. In some ways, I feel that's what we are living through again in America through our increasing economic divide where the anger and emotional response in our own democracy has led to a populist appeal to burn the system down. When something like this burns, the fire cannot necessarily be controlled, or the rage that comes together with it. I fear what is coming. I want US-Japan to be on the same side at least at the societal level, through organizations like Japan Society and all of the Japan-America Societies around the country that believe in the importance of Japan. I want us to speak out with one voice and also to help our friends in Japan understand that they do have agency and that their voices matter in the international conversation. It's not just Americans versus Americans. What happens in America has a global impact and what happens in the world has an impact on America.

INFLECTION POINT

We're at an inflection point where the rules don't seem to count anymore—or maybe the old rules are being rewritten before our eyes. The traditional mentality, which in Japan has often played out as passivity, as sitting back and waiting for the rules to be rewritten, isn't going to work now.

Japan has the opportunity to play a far more significant role in global leadership not simply by seeking a seat at traditional power tables like the United Nations Security Council—though inclusion there would be meaningful—but by helping to redefine what leadership itself looks like in the twenty-first century. This means leveraging its soft power not as decoration, but as a core diplomatic tool: showing how values like humility, long-term thinking, social cohesion, and respect for difference can guide international cooperation. Japan can lead on global challenges—like aging societies, climate adaptation, AI ethics, and disaster resilience—not by imposing models, but by offering thoughtful, culturally grounded approaches rooted in its own lived experience. It can convene unlikely partners, host global dialogues in distinctly Japanese spaces, and elevate voices often overlooked by traditional diplomacy. Being part of the global rewrite means Japan not only participates in shaping the rules—it helps reimagine the purpose and tone of global engagement itself.

If Japan fails to act—to assert its voice, share its values, and actively shape the global conversation—it risks becoming increasingly irrelevant in a world that is rapidly being redrawn. Soft power, like leadership itself, is not static; it must be exercised to be effective. If Japan remains overly cautious, inward-looking, or reliant on the protective framework of others, it will forfeit the influence it has earned through decades of peace, innovation, and cultural resonance. Others will fill the vacuum, setting standards and narratives that may not align with Japan's interests or values. Silence, in this moment of global transition, is not neutrality—it's retreat. To do nothing is not to preserve Japan's quiet strength, but to let it fade. This is a moment that demands intention, not passivity.

Some of the lessons that Japan has learned from the past, especially from the 1960s or 1980s, are no longer applicable and need to be discarded, perhaps even in favor of the 1860s. Global surveys and cultural metrics consistently underscore just how deeply Japan has become woven into daily life in America and beyond. A 2025 Global Soft Power Index placed Japan as the world's fourth most influential nation—ahead of Germany and the UK—while Yale's nineteen-country study found that most respondents view Japan favorably and "cool," especially in Asia and the Middle East.

In the US, Japan's cultural footprint has grown exponentially. Surveys consistently show that the majority of American Gen Z regularly watch anime, with platforms like Netflix pivoting to keep up with dedicated platforms such as Crunchyroll that has seen exponential growth in the last decade now reaching over fifteen million subscribers worldwide—most of whom engage daily and are dedicated consumers who buy related merchandise. What was once niche—like anime, manga, and Japanese fashion—has become mainstream: sixty-five percent of young anime fans say it's their go-to media. Hello Kitty and *kawaii* aesthetics influence fashion, and Japanese gaming icons appear in everyday American life through adoption by athletes and celebrities consistently. For younger generations, Japanese content and products aren't exotic curiosities—they're part of their lifestyles and identities in a way that was unimaginable in the twentieth century. Part of my argument here is that Japan is too often put into an Asian bucket, but that bucket is only relevant to America, not the Pacific or the Indo-Pacific. My own history has shown me that Japan is everywhere and that its presence is felt everywhere from Brazil to Kazakhstan.

In some ways the global perspective on US-Japan is not purely bilateral. Japan really is everywhere, and it only helps US-Japan to acknowledge that global perspective and not to pretend that there's a vacuum in which US-Japan relations have no outside impact. That is a fundamental flaw in the way that US-Japan has been taught and it is also the way I've experienced the emerging US-Japan space. We can find that new awareness once we actually jump into the new rules of the game.

NEW RULES, NEW GAME

It appears that America is no longer interested in being a global leader and is refocusing internally, leaving Japan behind in the US-dependent position it has occupied since the end of World War II. That is no longer to Japan's advantage. To join the new game, Japan urgently needs to articulate and define its own national interest, and it needs to do that on the global stage. While it is clear that Japan does have a national interest, it is rarely articulated in a very loud voice even within the country, and when used as an internal signaling mechanism it's certainly not something that outsiders can perceive. Part of what international relations teaches us is that if you don't signal, if you don't put your needs out there, that's how miscalculations and mistakes happen. If Japan isn't making its own national interests clear to outsiders, including maintaining regional stability in the Indo-Pacific, ensuring energy and economic security, upholding a rules-based international order, protecting its territorial integrity, and preserving its cultural identity while remaining globally competitive, how do the Japanese expect others to play the game? It won't be to Japan's advantage. No one thinks of Japan as a doormat. It's been seen throughout history that it is a very poor idea to try to provoke or take over Japan. Even after World War II, America, with all of its military force, never tried to colonize Japan while occupying it. The imperial system was left in place, along with the core of Japanese society, because there was a deep appreciation for Japan in America even if the two countries had been mortal enemies during the war.

The reshaping of Japan in a global context is long overdue. What I want is for Japan to reshape itself not by abandoning its postwar identity, but by evolving it—stepping into a more proactive, confident role on the global stage that reflects its true capabilities and values. This means moving beyond the constraints of a reactive, US-dependent foreign policy and embracing a bolder, more independent strategic identity. The Japanese constitution, particularly Article 9, which renounces war and prohibits maintaining military forces for conflict, has long symbolized Japan's pacifism. But today, I believe Japan must reinterpret—not necessarily abolish—Article 9 to allow for a realistic and responsible defense posture that protects its interests and contributes meaningfully to global peace. This would include clearer legal authority for collective self-defense, deeper regional security cooperation, and a more transparent dialogue with its citizens about the role of the Self-Defense Forces. It's not about remilitarization; it's about redefinition—making Japan a more active shaper of world affairs rather than a passive observer, grounded in its own values but no longer limited by outdated assumptions.

Whether it concerns the Japanese constitution or just Article 9 on Japan's military and its ability to fight a war, a conversation needs to be happening without the taboos of the past. Something else to discuss is Japan's nuclear capabilities, another taboo topic in Japan. If South Korea acquires a nuclear weapon, Japan will feel it has no choice but to develop its own in order to maintain strategic balance, deter regional threats, and preserve its national security credibility amid a rapidly shifting Northeast Asian security landscape. Japan's security can't be discussed without talking about nuclear fission, whether nuclear energy or weapons, at some point in the future. That's not something the Japanese want to think about, especially after 3.11. Ultimately this isn't about what happens to the US—Japan needs to articulate clearly that it wants to control its own destiny. Part of that control is its relationship with the US, which is always going to be the most important. The question is, will that relationship be important for the right reasons? I can see a scenario where if the US goes too far with its inward tilt, Japan will feel that it has no choice but to try to balance America's isolationism, just like what happened in the 1920s. I worry that that analogy doesn't lead to a positive outcome, and that if we forget our history, we're doomed to repeat it in some ways.

THE PRESENT MOMENT

There's a certain stability inherent in examining past history in the context of a contemporary narrative. Present history, however, is no longer stable. We're living through a turning point that is most likely a once-in-eighty-years instance, something that I would not have necessarily acknowledged when I began writing this book. The second Trump administration is bringing about fundamental changes to the US, and thereby, to US-Japan and the world, that cannot simply be ignored. It's impossible to say now that Americans didn't know what they were getting with the 2024 elections. The present moment reflects something much larger and much more urgent. The question we all need to ask now is why is Japan still so passive on the global stage? Why is the US-Japan community not acting with a sense of urgency or even positioning itself for the future?

It's incumbent on all of us in the US-Japan space to express this and it is also something that I am uniquely positioned to say as president and CEO of Japan Society. I also believe that the US-Japan relationship should not be only in the hands of the elites—the presidents and prime ministers, and all of the very high-level senior people who have traditionally respected what's been accomplished between our two nations. Traditionally, the term that's been used here is US-Japan "alliance managers," which in and of itself has elitist overtones. I don't even believe that a group of elites are in charge or may even exist any more. In some ways, Japan Society is another example of an elite institution that is promoting art and culture at the upper end of the spectrum while interest in Japan has actually been burgeoning at the pop culture level. Pop culture transcends all arts and economic levels to build a bridge into the abundance of Japan. It's a bridge that no one can build a wall around, one that unites us all—as global citizens, as Americans and Japanese—and it's something that makes us stronger by bringing us together. Japan's soft power is its greatest strength, and it will define the next generation in ways that the current elite cannot seem to fully understand.

CODA

I need to end this book by returning to *dosanko*, which puts my own journey as an insider and an outsider front and center in telling the story of how I became one of the US-Japan elite. Being one of the US-Japan elite is not a place where I feel comfortable, and I don't want to become stuck here in a sense of complacency where I am just protecting my own territory. I want the next generation to be able to come to Japan Society to experience the abundance of Japan. I want people beyond the far east side of Midtown Manhattan to experience what I have the privilege of experiencing every day at Japan House, both virtually and through partnerships. I want to see what the next Japan Society presidents and directors will do and those who follow them. I know that they will do things I cannot even imagine today just like my own predecessors have alongside our pivot during the pandemic and my own tenure. History shows us that institutions outlive their leaders and that nobody is indispensable. That's true for our democracies as well. Presidents and prime ministers come and go, but we, the people, ultimately get to shape our own stories and narratives. Part of that is by being an active citizen in our own democracies, as we've already talked about.

My whole life, my guiding philosophy has always come from Jeremiah 29:11: "'For I know the plans I have for you,' declares the Lord, 'plans to prosper you and not to harm you, plans to give you hope and a future.'" Because I have that sense of connectedness and optimism about the future, no matter how dark the world may be, I'm always going to look for something greater. If I can't find it in the American political process, I will find it in the American nonprofit sector. And if I can't find it in the American nonprofit sector, I'll find it in Japan, or Türkiye, or Kazakhstan, all of the places to which I've been connected. How do I help other people see parts of themselves in a story that is so different and so unique? What I hope to do here is to break the barriers to help us find our human connections, and to explain on many different levels how Americans and Japanese are dealing with the world they live in. In this way we can achieve greater mutual understanding. All of these pieces, though, lead to the same thing, which is not to tell you what to do but to ask you to listen to your better angels and give people the benefit of the doubt, and to help people understand that in many ways they're actually more similar than different.

IN CONCLUSION

As I look back on this journey—both personal and geopolitical—I am struck by how much is still unwritten in the story of Japan and the United States. This book began with a deeply personal motivation: to make sense of my own life between two worlds and to offer that story as a bridge for others navigating the same. But it ends with a call—a plea, really—for a more expansive vision of what Japan can be in the world and how the US-Japan relationship can serve as a global model not just of alliance, but of co-creation.

Japan is no longer just a student of the international system, nor should it see itself as a junior partner to any power. The time has come for Japan to step forward—not as a replacement for America, but as a different kind of leader. One that draws on its soft power, cultural depth, and unique history of resilience to offer the world a model of leadership grounded not in dominance but in dignity. Whether through reimagining Article 9, investing in people-to-people diplomacy, or reinterpreting its pacifism for a new era of proactive peacebuilding, Japan must now take up its responsibility as a steward of global stability.

This moment requires not more noise, but more meaning. Not grandstanding, but intentionality. Not isolation, but interconnection. In a world increasingly fractured by division and exhausted by extremes, the quiet strength of Japan—and institutions like Japan Society—has never been more needed. Our mission now is to go beyond the *genkan*, beyond the ceremonial bow, and into the deeper rooms of relationship, mutual learning, and shared destiny.

If I've learned anything from growing up in Hokkaido and standing at the intersection of these two cultures, it's that the real work of bridge-building happens not on stages or in headlines, but in quiet moments of trust, understanding, and return. That is the space I hope this book opens—and the spirit I hope we all carry forward together.

AFTERWORD

The quiet ritual of a Japanese green tea ceremony has always struck me as more than just a cultural practice—it is a metaphor for the work of bridge-building and life itself. Every movement is deliberate, every gesture imbued with respect, every moment shared between host and guest meant to create harmony. In the stillness of that exchange, centuries of tradition flow into the present, reminding us that true connection is never rushed. As I bring this book to a close, I think of that ceremony: a pause to reflect, to honor those who have come before, and to prepare thoughtfully for what lies ahead in the story of US-Japan relations.

When I started writing this book, I wasn't quite sure who would be interested in reading it. Now, at the other end of the process, I am grateful for the story it tells and the messages that I hope will resonate throughout each of the chapters. *Beyond the Genkan* is not just about me and my individual story, it's about how a particular set of circumstances in one person's life can take on meaning in a greater context.

One of the challenges we have with US-Japan relations is that it is hard to personify. There is usually the American perspective, as seen through the lens of the American president, or the Japanese perspective, usually the Japanese prime minister. Here I've turned this concept upside down and stood it on its head from the perspective of a *dosanko* American who is not only a global citizen and a scholar of geopolitics but also a leader in the US-Japan space. That's what is unique about this book, which brings something to life that I've never seen before, and it is only partly because my own personal history is so unique.

My deepest hope in writing this book is that it will serve as more than just a personal narrative or a historical account—it will be a resource for all who believe in the power of bridge-building. The US-Japan relationship has never been static; it has evolved through war, reconciliation, and renewal into one of the most resilient partnerships in the world. Yet, for this partnership to remain strong, it must be continually nurtured by people who see its potential not only in diplomacy or economics, but in culture, education, technology, and human connection.

Throughout this book are what my dad would call "golden nuggets"—universal principles named after the lessons I learned as a pastor's child. These are not only the core principles that have guided US-Japan over the eighty years following the end of World War II but also other viewpoints that I hope can be used as the foundation for the next decades of US-Japan.

I hope that the case studies, reflections, and lessons captured in these pages inspire you, the reader, to think boldly about how we can contribute together. We all have something to offer. Whether through public service, entrepreneurship, cultural exchange, or quiet acts of friendship, each of us holds the power to shape this vital partnership. If even a few readers come away from this book with a renewed commitment to strengthening the bonds between our two nations and societies, then I will consider this effort a success.

As America's global role and alliances become increasingly transactional, Japan can no longer rely on the United States as its sole strategic anchor. The modern US-Japan relationship that was renewed eighty years ago must now be fundamentally recast because the world in which that alliance was brought to fruition no longer exists, even at a time when Japan's appeal has never been higher. Drawing on its soft power, strong markets, and social harmony, Japan needs to define and act in its own national interest. The US-Japan relationship is more than a treaty, it is a living connection between two democracies, bound by shared values and a commitment to openness in a time when the world is moving toward division.

The US-Japan alliance has weathered storms before, and it will undoubtedly face new challenges ahead. But if we continue to invest in people, to share our stories honestly, and to see in each other both our differences and our shared humanity, I am confident that the bridge between our nations will stand stronger than ever.

The election of Sanae Takaichi as LDP president and Japan's first female prime minister marks a historic turning point that perfectly underscores the themes of this book. As a protégé of the late Prime Minister Shinzo Abe, she inherits both his legacy and a deeply complicated political landscape—one that will test many of the propositions explored here. Whether she endures like her mentor or fades like her rival Shigeru Ishiba, her leadership will reveal much about Japan's evolving political identity amid growing divides between Nagatachō and the heartland, mirroring those between Washington and America's own. Managing her relationship with President Trump beyond their first meeting will be necessary but not sufficient to sustaining the US-Japan alliance, which now belongs not only to leaders but to citizens, companies, and communities on both sides of the Pacific. Yet as I have argued throughout, the real story lies not in the headlines of summits, but in the deeper human connections that bind Japan and

America—from businesses and classrooms to baseball fields and cultural exchanges. If Japan can bring its spirit of *omotenashi*—anticipating needs before they are spoken—to this relationship, then this new chapter may become not only a test but an opportunity. It is precisely at such thresholds, or *genkans*, that we must decide whether to hesitate at the doorway or step forward into a shared future.

This book is for everyone who cares deeply about the US-Japan relationship, whether your interest is personal, cultural, or professional. By inviting you, the reader, into my life and beyond the *genkan* in the context of US-Japan I am opening up my own sacred space, the equivalent of sharing a bowl of tea together in the interests of peace, harmony, and mutual understanding. Let's make the most of our time together.

ACKNOWLEDGMENTS

This book could not have come to life without the support, encouragement, and wisdom of so many. First and foremost, I am deeply grateful to my family—Megan, Jack, and Macy, plus Carlton, Cornelia, and Chris along with our extended family from New York, Virginia, Florida, Kentucky, and beyond—whose patience, love, and belief in me have sustained this journey from the very beginning.

Beyond my biological family I've been blessed with many other families from the churches I grew up with in Japan from Sapporo Baptist to Living Hope Church to professionally wherever I have lived and work.

There are far too many mentors, colleagues, and friends to name them all, but let me at least acknowledge here as best I can those who have most profoundly shaped this journey. From my earliest days as a Fulbright Scholar in Türkiye, where Professor Hüseyin Bağcı at the Middle East Technical University took me in as family and taught me the human side of international affairs, to my years as a young professional in

Washington, DC, at the German Marshall Fund, the State Department, APCO Worldwide, the USA Pavilion in Kazakhstan, and later Eurasia Group, Japan Society, and the many other places that shaped me in between, I have been blessed with mentors who believed in me before I believed in myself. My former bosses and still mentors—Ian Bremmer, Margery Kraus, Heidi Crebo-Rediker, Karen Donfried, Craig Kennedy, Stephen Szabo and Eric Edelman —each modeled leadership rooted in purpose and integrity.

At Princeton, scholars like Ezra Suleiman, Aaron Friedberg, John Ikenberry, Gilbert Rozman, Michael Reynolds, Daniel Kliman, and Michael McKoy deepened my understanding of academia and international relations. At Yale, Paul Kennedy, John Gaddis, and Charlie Hill in the Grand Strategy Program along with my fellow students taught me to think across centuries, not news cycles, while at the University of Tokyo, professors Kiichi Fujiwara, Shinichi Kitaoka, Akihiko Tanaka, Ryo Sahashi, and Lully Miura helped me see Japan's diplomacy through both historical and human lenses. And at the University of Richmond, mentors such as Doug Hicks, the broader Jepson faculty, Uliana Gabara, John Outland, and all of my international studies friends encouraged me to believe that ideas can move people, and people can move history.

I am particularly indebted to dear friends who are more like brothers that encouraged me at every step: Jonathan Zur, Britt Yamamoto, Tomoaki Ishigaki and Aaron Graham foremost among them. Each offered not only insight, but also the gift of believing in the importance of this work when I needed it most.

At Japan Society, I owe a special debt of gratitude to our remarkable team, whose dedication inspires me every day. In particular, Justin Rockefeller, who first convinced me to take on this leadership role along with our Chair Merit Janow, past Chairs Joseph Perella and Wilbur Ross, along with all of our committed board members past and present along with our staff among whom I have to single out Cynthia Sternau, who played an instrumental role in shaping this book—her guidance and steady hand were invaluable in bringing these pages to life. Lastly, I'd like to thank the entire board and staff of Japan Society for the privilege of leading this almost 120-year-old organization in a mission that is critical for the future of US-Japan and deeply personal to me.

To all of you—colleagues, friends, mentors, and family—thank you for helping me find my voice in these pages and for reminding me why this story matters.

ABOUT THE AUTHOR

JOSHUA W. WALKER, PHD, is president and CEO of Japan Society. He has held leadership positions at Eurasia Group, the USA Pavilion of the 2017 World Expo, and APCO Worldwide, previously serving in the State Department and the Defense Department.

He is Senior Fellow at the Center for the Study of the Presidency and Congress, Adjunct Associate Professor of International and Public Affairs at Columbia University, Presidential Leadership Scholar, David Rockefeller Fellow of the Trilateral Commission, Munich Security Conference Young Leader, British-American Project Fellow, and Nakasone Yasuhiro Award Winner. He was previously a Professor of Leadership and the American Presidency at George Mason University and the Reagan Foundation, Transatlantic Fellow at the German Marshall Fund of the United States, and cofounder of the *Yale Journal of International Affairs*.

He holds a bachelor's degree from the University of Richmond, a master's degree from Yale University, and a doctorate from Princeton University.

in drjwalk

@drjoshuawalker

joshua.w.walker.5

𝕏 @drjwalk